Managing the Primary School

Tim Hill

David Fulton Publishers
London

David Fulton Publishers Ltd
2 Barbon Close, Great Ormond Street, London WC1N 3JX

First published in Great Britain by
David Fulton Publishers 1989

British Library Cataloguing in Publication Data

Hill, Tim
Managing the Primary School
1. Great Britain. Primary schools.
Management
I. Title
372.12'00941

ISBN 1-85346-096-6

Typeset by Chapterhouse, Formby

Printed in Great Britain by A. Wheaton & Co., Ltd., Exeter

Contents

Foreword

Twenty years after the publication of the Plowden Report seemed to be a proper and conventional time for some assessment of the state of affairs in Primary Schooling, and the series of which this volume is a member arose from such a consideration. Powerful in its presentation and comprehensive in its coverage, the Plowden Report was also distinctive. Previous reports on education appeared to rely mainly upon their Committee's sampling of presumed informed opinion for their recommendations. In contrast, the Plowden Committee conducted national surveys to obtain answers to some of its questions. The authors of the report attempted to portray the psychological development of the child as a frame of reference to which to relate the curriculum. Alas, this precedent of establishing a sound research base on which to found educational decisions has not been the hallmark of subsequent government policies. Neither has there been a systematic review of Plowden's proposals and assumptions.

Perhaps it is instructive to reacall how little space Plowden devoted to management. The report had much to say about children and curriculum whereas there is an assumption and preference that management could and should be minimal. Unseen hands were to be preferred to explicit procedures. Certainly there was no strong demand for the training of Primary Heads and, as Tim Hill writes, such an absence presupposes that good management requires no more than thoughtful and intelligent commonsense. Since Plowden, however, the issue of management has grown *à la Gargantua*.

In part, this growth has been occasioned by a growth in the responsibilities assigned to Headteachers. The Plowden philosophy that education has to be of and for the *whole* child has likewise widened the Headteacher's purview when this has been translated into practice.

The too many changes inflicted upon Primary Schools in the last two decades have added to the managerial burden. These are real additions to the role of Head.

In part, however, I fear that the growth in concern about management has affinities with Parkinson's principles; perhaps the rhetoric of management has increased geometrically, whilst the tasks have increased only arithmetically. Likewise, some of the perfectly satisfactory practices previously pursued by competent individuals have been transformed into rituals of consultation, which often seem to require the setting up of working parties, committees or meetings.

Not all change is progress. Neither could it yet be claimed that the growth of management training has been accompanied by a corresponding growth in knowledge about management. The foundations of management training are at worst unrelated to such base disciplines as psychology and sociology. Fortunately and sensibly, Tim Hill avoids the potential pitfalls. He does not discuss the extent to which Heads have become victims of too much rhetoric and ritual, neither does he himself use too much of the jargon currently in vogue. He does not ask questions about or regret the absence of underpinning theory. Heads have to act today and cannot wait for theory to be developed and substantiated. They have to cope with the current legislation as of now.

Tim Hill offers immediate aid. Revising his pre-publication text as legislation passed through parliament, Tim Hill presents the contemporary tasks of Primary Heads. His discussion of ways of handling these tasks is in simple English. The advice he offers for successful performance of these tasks is practical. Where possible, it is founded upon empirical evidence derived from systematic research. Where that is not to hand, Tim Hill relies on the precedents of the accumulated experiences of the many Primary Heads he has encountered in the course of his own career as practitioner and trainer.

If it is permissible to resurrect a pre-Plowden injunction, may I suggest that it will be greatly to the advantage of all Primary Heads to read, mark, learn and inwardly digest this text? It may help to render their difficult and demanding roles somewhat easier.

Peter Robinson
January 1989

Introduction

> A good headteacher is the closest thing to a 'magic wand' for a primary school, said Sir Keith Joseph, in evidence to the Commons Select Committee on Education. *Times Educational Supplement* 11 April 1986, p.10

Sir Keith was here voicing a widely-held view about the importance of the headteacher. Parents, teachers, governors, education officers, HMI - and children too - all know that the quality of the head is the single most important factor in determining the quality of the school. Support for this popular view has recently come from a major study of school effectiveness (Mortimore *et al.*, 1988). There was already an abundance of evidence from school effectiveness studies around the world, but most notably from the USA, that the popular view was right. Nor is this view of the head anything new. The 'Headmaster Tradition' has its roots in the nineteenth-century public school as Baron (1974) has shown. Perhaps it was appropriate for the Secretary of State to be reaffirming the centrality of the headteacher in primary school management in view of his Prime Minister's endorsement of a return to 'Victorian values'.

In the current climate, however, the image of the successful headteacher is very different from that of his Victorian predecessor. The headteacher now is a manager rather than an autocrat. He may still need charisma to enlist support for his 'mission' for the school but the style has changed markedly. School management has drawn to some extent on mainstream management in commercial and public service organisations. Particularly influential has been the vogue for examining successful organisations so that other less successful ones may emulate their features. In this field Peters and Waterman's investigation of America's top companies, *In Search of Excellence* (1982) has been seminal. In fact their book was so successful, not least in terms of financial reward, that it spawned a host of books by other authors with the word 'excellence' in their titles.

The message, substantiated by the school effectiveness studies, has been spread widely in the USA by writers such as Sergiovanni:

> Successful schools seem to have strong and functional cultures aligned with a vision of excellence in schooling. This culture serves as a compass setting to steer people in a common direction; provides a set of norms that defines what people should accomplish and how; and provides a source of meaning and significance for teachers, students, administrators, and others as they work . . . Strong functional cultures . . . are nurtured and built by the school leadership and membership.
>
> (Sergiovanni, 1984)

Seen from this angle a key part of the head's job is to establish a strong culture which promotes excellence. Deal also takes the lessons learned from studies of successful companies and applies them to schools:

> Behind effective schools, like high-performing businesses, there is a strong culture that encourages productivity, high morale, confidence, and commitment. Making schools more effective requires building and reshaping the hidden, taken-for-granted rules that govern day-to-day behavior.
>
> (Deal, 1985)

One must be wary of extrapolating findings from commerce too readily and applying them to schools. Primary schools might resemble Marks and Spencer or General Motors in certain ways, but they also differ from these organisations and the differences are more significant than the similarities. However, studies like Mortimore *et al.*, (1988), which was carried out in English junior schools, and the American studies of effective schools and principals have told us a great deal about what it is that effective headteachers do in their effective schools. **Effective heads differ from less effective heads in the way that they manage their schools**. While not wishing to give the erroneous impression that school improvement is just a matter of analysing what effective heads do and then applying those maxims to any and every situation, there is clearly much that heads can learn from studying how effective heads manage their schools.

Yet the study of management has only relatively recently become an acceptable thing for primary heads to do. Only ten years ago when I was given a half-day's leave from my job as a primary head to take an Open University exam in school management, my local Senior

Education Officer was puzzled and could not understand why I should want to study such a subject. He himself had never bothered with such things and believed that any fair-minded, well-educated, reasonable person could 'fly a school by the seat of his pants'. I always feel reassured when I climb into a jumbo jet that British Airways does not share his philosophy. Surely parents, who are required to entrust the life chances of their most precious possessions to headteachers, are entitled to at least the same reassurance that I demand as an air passenger: that the guy up-front knows what he is doing.

Some of the doubts about school management are based upon a misconception of what it has to offer. This is partly due to the extravagant claims made for management in earlier days, and to the dubious methods which its proponents advocated. What is discussed in this book is not a set of management techniques designed completely to eliminate uncertainty, complexity and ambiguity from what is always going to be an uncertain and messy activity (the 'hyper-rational school' of management). Nor does the book offer a sure-fire way of bending everyone to one's will (the 'macho school' of management); the days of the 'heroic' head have gone, although some of the heroes seem not to have realised this.

Instead the approach is one which is more in tune with the inherently and attractively informal nature of a primary school; one which seeks to enhance teachers' professionality rather than to diminish it. The approach is intended to be more systematic than normal current primary management practice so that the school may be run more effectively in order to enhance the quality of education that its pupils experience. Even the goal of enhancing teachers' working lives has that same ulterior motive of improving the educational experience of children. The school exists for the children rather than the teachers. Fortunately the vast majority of teachers find their greatest source of job satisfaction in the knowledge that the children are achieving their potential in a warm and supportive environment, so there is no inherent contradiction between the aims of an effective primary school and the interests of the professional primary teacher.

Indeed there has probably never been a more challenging time for headteachers in this country, no time when the need for sensitive management skills has been greater. It has become a cliché to observe that we live in times of rapid change. Cliché it may be, but it is nonetheless true. Control of our state school system is being simultaneously centralised and devolved in a way that is likely to transform it, for good or ill. It is ironic that a great number of centrally controlled systems of education around the world were established under colonial rule by Britain and in almost every one there are moves afoot to decentralise control. Educationists from many of these countries are puzzled by our new-found enthusiasm for something with which they have become dissatisfied. As a result of the combined effects of the 1986 and 1988 Education Acts, all serving heads, and most teachers, will shortly find themselves operating in a school system which is radically different from the one which they were originally motivated to enter. The ground rules are changing as the system becomes both more centrally controlled and more 'client-led', as the jargon has it. Heads will face problems of readjustment themselves but so will their staff. So, not only must heads cope with their own adjustment problems, but they will need to facilitate the adjustment of their teachers as well, or the children in our schools will be the losers, which is an unacceptable outcome for all.

School management is about school improvement, and various techniques, trends and approaches exist which together could make that claim a reality. School development plans, staff development policies, school review, local financial management, staff appraisal for development, improved continuity, more effective staff selection procedures, increased parental involvement, increased governor involvement – all offer ways of improving the school. In order actually to fulfil that potential they all need to be approached in similar ways which stress cooperation, trust, openness, participation, reflection, professionalism, commitment to high standards of achievement and a determination to solve problems. There are no easy answers to managing an effective primary school, as Huberman and Miles observed of American schools:

> School improvement is a messy, rich process full of coercion and shared struggle, indifference and heavy involvement, uncertain results and real payoffs.
>
> (Huberman and Miles, 1984, p.1)

There is a large element of faith, as Acker (1988) pointed out, in the primary teachers' job. When the children leave the school they are still immature and their teachers do not know how those children will turn out as mature adults. It is significant that one of the favourite topics of staffroom conversation in a school with a stable staff is that of ex-pupils and their achievements. Such pieces of news can confirm the teacher's faith that although they rarely see the final result of their work it has indeed been worthwhile. In other words, there can be a real payoff to all that shared struggle and heavy involvement.

Overview of the book

The first part of the book is concerned with relating the school to its changing environment. This is an environment which includes the now very powerful governing body. Newly constituted governing bodies will represent the interests of the various stakeholders in the school: parents; staff; LEA; and the wider community in which the school is located. Chapter 2 focuses on the relationship between the school and the children's parents. Here there are developments both in terms of involving parents more in the decision-making processes and in participating much more in the teaching of their own children. Chapter 3 examines the changing relationship with the Local Education Authority (LEA). Here there are contradictory trends as the power of the LEA is reduced by the Education Reform Act while the advisory services become more inspectorial as they assume the role of policing the National Curriculum. The relationship, such as it is, with the Department of Education and Science is the subject of Chapter 4. The main concern here is with the role of Her Majesty's Inspectorate of Schools, the so-called 'eyes and ears' of the Department, who have actual contact with the schools.

Having considered the environment within which the school must operate, the focus of the book then switches to the internal processes of the school, which are all seen in terms of enhancing the quality of the children's educational experience. Chapter 5 looks at the role of the head in the light of recent knowledge about effective school leadership. This leads to a consideration in Chapter 6 of how heads manage that most precious of scarce resources: their own time. Chapter 7 examines the management of the curriculum and concludes that, even with the implementation of a National Curriculum, this will continue to be a central task of school management. The management of financial resources, covered in Chapter 8, has become a much more important topic for heads. With the arrival of delegated budgets in primary schools the notion that finances somehow manage themselves is no longer sustainable. The management of change, which is the subject of Chapter 9, is a central task for school management and one where there are many relevant insights available from recent work in this field. Chapter 10 looks at the question of how schools can improve the continuity of children's learning, particularly as they move from one phase of schooling to the next. Chapter 11 examines ways in which the staff of a school can evaluate the work of the school and plan for its development.

The final two chapters focus specifically upon the staff of the school.

Chapter 12 examines ways in which the process of appointing staff to the school might be improved. This is a topic which has special relevance when one considers the length of time that a member of staff may remain in one school. Chapter 13 considers how the head may plan for the professional development of the teachers in the school. Recent developments here in the form of devolved INSET budgets and 'Baker Days' mean that a school with a systematic staff development policy can plan a programme to meet the identified needs of both the school and of its teachers, in order to enhance its effectiveness.

CHAPTER 1

Relationships with the Governing Body

Many new heads have had little real contact with a governing body apart from being interviewed by one. It it not surprising therefore that they should feel considerable uncertainty in establishing a relationship with the governors of their new school. What is the role of the governing body? What are its responsibilities? What are its powers? How much should the governors be told? How much should the head try to involve all of the governors in the life of the school?

These are just a few of the questions which new heads face in establishing their relationship with their governing body. One in eight of Weindling and Earley's (1987) new secondary heads admitted to a lack of preparation in this area of headship. Interestingly, 29 per cent of the LEA officers, who in many cases had opportunities to observe heads in this part of their job, picked out the relationship with governors as an area of headship for which heads were ill-prepared. However, it is not only new heads who find this relationship problematic. Recent legislation has so radically altered the composition, role, responsibilities and power of governing bodies that even experienced heads are finding that they are entering uncharted territory. Nor is it only headteachers who are uncertain. Even before the recent legislative changes Kogan *et al.* (1984) found that governors themselves were just as uncertain about the part they were expected to play.

After spending the previous three years studying school governing bodies, Maurice Kogan and his team concluded that:

> . . . at the present time school governing bodies are 'Sleeping Beauties' still awaiting the kiss of politics.
>
> (Kogan *et al.*, 1984, p.9)

Their conclusion still holds true though Prince Charming is already pursing his lips. It remains to be seen how far the combined effects of the 1986 and 1988 Education Acts manage to rouse school governing bodies from their traditionally reactive role so that they transform themselves into the proactive controllers of the school which the legislation envisages.

Kogan's study is the only substantial piece of research on this topic carried out within the last twenty years or so; although it pre-dates the recent legislative changes, I shall still be drawing upon his findings and upon his discussion of the issues, supplemented wherever possible by the somewhat scant evidence on the effects of the 1986 Act.

HISTORICAL BACKGROUND

Governing bodies have a history almost as long as that of schooling itself. They have their origins in the boards of trustees that administered the charity schools which preceded the involvement of the state in the provision of schools. The voluntary schools established by the National Society and the British and Foreign School Society were governed by boards of managers, who raised money for the school, employed its staff and generally supervised all aspects of the running of the school. The elementary schools established by the new school boards following the 1870 Education Act also, for the most part, had boards of managers with varying degrees of power to run the school.

The Cross Commission endorsed the system of school management committees in its Final Report of 1888. The Commission saw managers as contributing to the running of the school in such matters as the hiring and firing of teachers and the provision of equipment. In order to discharge these responsibilities managers would need, in addition to a 'general zeal for education', both 'business habits' and 'administrative ability'. However, the Commission saw the managers' role as more extensive than mere administration; managers would also have an influence over the pupils in order to:

> . . . mould their character, and help to make them good and useful members of society.
>
> (Cross Report, 1888)

This would be achieved by visiting the school frequently and for this task the manager would need:

> . . . some amount of education, tact, interest in school work, a sympathy with the teachers and scholars, to which may be added residence in reasonable proximity to the school, together with leisure time during school hours . . . and it is hardly necessary to say that personal oversight of the religious and moral instruction implies religious character in those who are to exercise it.
>
> (Cross Report, 1888)

It comes as little surprise to learn from Gordon (1974) that managing bodies were almost entirely middle class in their composition. In London he found that 31 per cent came from the 'leisured classes', 21 per cent from the churches and 10 per cent from the professions. Elementary schools, whether provided by a school board or a voluntary society, were provided for working class children by the middle class. The teachers who worked in them were drawn largely, like the children they taught, from the working class, and the board of managers was thus an important control mechanism intended to ensure that elementary schooling did nothing which would challenge the existing distribution of power and wealth in Victorian Britain. Whatever the motivation of individual educators, mass public elementary education was never intended by the legislators to threaten the status quo, but rather to reinforce it.

The 1902 Education Act, which established Local Education Authorities, required all but the smallest LEAs to appoint boards of managers for their schools. A number of LEAs appointed managing bodies for groups of elementary schools; in some cases that group comprised all of the elementary schools in the authority, thus retaining close and direct control of the schools in the hands of the LEA itself. Subsequent legislation continued, with only minor changes, the basic pattern of managing bodies which had become established in the nineteenth century.

When the Taylor Committee began its study of managing and governing bodies in 1975 it found that they had evolved over the years to produce:

> . . . a bewildering variety of practice and opinion . . .
>
> (Taylor Report, 1977)

Their report was greeted by much consternation on the part of the teaching unions, who saw any extension, or revival, of governing bodies' powers as a threat to the autonomy of heads and teachers. The Committee produced eighty-nine recommendations for the reform of school governing bodies, which were intended to produce a mechanism whereby:

> . . . all the parties concerned for a school's success – the local education authority, the staff, the parents and the local community – should be brought together so that they can discuss, debate and justify the proposals which any one of them may seek to implement.
>
> (Taylor Report, 1977)

Their intention was reflected in the title of their report: *A New Partner-*

ship For Our Schools. Every school should have its own governing body composed of representatives drawn equally from the LEA, the staff, the community and the parents. This body would have clearly defined, but wide ranging, powers to control all school policy decisions. The recommendations on membership were controversial at the time not only because they included equal representation for parents but because the LEA would lose its majority on the new, more powerful governing bodies.

The Education Act 1980, which was not fully implemented until 1985, embodied only token versions of the Taylor recommendations. It required all governing bodies to include representatives of both the teaching staff and of the parents. Headteachers were given the right to be governors of their own school if they so chose, but the LEAs were allowed to retain a majority of their own nominees on each governing body. It ended the use of the term ‘managing body’ for primary schools; largely ended the practice of grouping schools under joint governing bodies; insisted that minutes should be open to the public; and limited the number of governing bodies upon which any individual might sit. However, it remained silent upon the subject of the functions and powers of governing bodies.

The Green Paper *Parental Influence at School* (1984) suggested two major changes in the law relating to school government:

> . . . first that parents elected by their fellow parents in a secret ballot should be able to form the majority on the governing bodies of county and maintained special schools . . . second, that appropriate powers for governing bodies should be entrenched by legislation so that these could not, as can happen at present, be overridden by the LEA.
>
> (DES, *Better Schools*, 1985, p.64)

The reaction to the proposal to give parents a majority was so hostile, with even such bodies as the National Confederation of Parent Teacher Associations opposing it, that the subsequent legislation, the Education (No.2) Act 1986, did not include any such provision. It is this Act which provides the current statutory framework for school government – a framework which seeks to limit the power of the LEAs in the control of schools by increasing that of parents and of the community, and which largely eliminates the ‘bewildering variety of practice’ which the Taylor Committee noted.

THE CURRENT POSITION

The current statutory framework for school government is provided by the 1986 Education (No.2) Act and the Education Reform Act 1988.

Taken together these measures substantially increase the power of governing bodies, largely at the expense of the LEA rather than of the head.

i Composition of the governing body

The composition of the governing body of each school is intended to ensure that '. . . no single interest will predominate' (*Better Schools*, DES, 1985). Thus none of the partners (LEA, staff, parents, community) has a majority on the governing body. Additionally the annual meeting of parents is intended to strengthen the parents' influence on the governors. The composition of governing bodies is given in the table.

Composition of Governing Bodies for County and Controlled Schools

Size	Parents	LEA	Head	Teachers	Co-opted/Foundation	Total
⟨100	2	2	1	1	3 (1/2)	9
100 – 299	3	3	1	1	4 (1/3)	12
⟩300*	4	4	1	2	5 (1/4)	16
⟩600*	5	5	1	2	6 (2/4)	19

*instruments of government may specify either

Source: DES Circular 8/86

ii Governors and the curriculum

The 1986 Act gave significantly greater responsibilities to the governing body for determining the curriculum, but these have been modified and reduced by the 1988 Act. The establishment of a National Curriculum reduces the scope for governors to participate in the decision-making concerning what should be taught in the school. The LEA is required to determine its policy for the secular curriculum in all the schools which it maintains and this policy must include all the statutory elements of the National Curriculum. The governing body of each school must define the secular curriculum for the school in the light of the LEA's policy and the requirements of the National Curriculum. In doing this the governors must consult the headteacher and the LEA if they propose to modify the LEA's policy. The head is then required to implement the governors' curriculum policy in the school. The governors have a responsibility to ensure that the National Curriculum is followed. Whether sex education is to be included in the school's curriculum is to be determined by the governing body, but where it is they must ensure that it encourages '. . . the pupils to have due regard to moral considerations and the value of family life'. The governors also share with the head and the LEA a responsibility for ensuring that the 'junior pupils' do not engage in any partisan political activities in school and that no teachers promote partisan political views in their teaching. These provisions were the result of amendments during the passage of the 1986 Act and their interpretation has yet to be defined by the courts; until that happens their precise meaning is by no means easy to see. Nor is it easy to see exactly how governing bodies will use their power to modify the LEA's curriculum policy, but the requirement to follow the National Curriculum leaves little room for local variation, which was of course the Secretary of State's intention. It seems likely that governors will in practice do little more than discuss the relative time allocations to different subjects within the National Curriculum. The arrangements for testing pupils' progress will give them a new source of data which they will be able to use to monitor the effectiveness of the school. This will involve the head in an educative task vis-à-vis the governors if they are to appreciate both the limitations of testing and the caution with which such results should be interpreted.

iii The governors' report to parents

The governors are required by the 1986 Education Act to prepare and send to the pupils' parents an annual report, which must include certain factual information about the school and its governing body but should consist mainly of a summary of the steps taken by the governors in the discharge of their functions over the previous year.

The National Foundation for Educational Research (NFER) organised a conference in 1988 after the first round of governors' reports and annual parents' meetings, at which the findings of several small-scale studies were reported (Earley, 1988). The picture conveyed by these studies, while consistent, is far from encouraging. However, in view of the fact that all of the studies were based on governors' first attempts at writing annual reports, one should be cautious about censuring these initial efforts.

Who pays?

Whether or not LEAs provided additional help with the preparation of annual reports seems to depend mostly upon whom one asks. 43 of the 52 LEAs that responded to the NFER School Governors Research Group enquiry on this subject claimed to have given additional help. Arden asked the schools within the London Diocesan Board for Schools the same question and found that 4 of the 11 LEAs gave no additional help. In Division 9 of ILEA, Buglione found that 25 per cent of the chairs of governors had paid for the report out of their own pockets.

Who writes the report?

According to the members of the National Association of Governors and Managers (NAGM) who attended their four conferences, reported by Kelly, the favoured arrangement is for a sub-committee representing the various interests on the governing body to prepare the initial draft with the help of the head. Bristow found that, in the secondary schools which he surveyed, this was done in 17 per cent of the schools. In 24 per cent the chair wrote the first draft alone, in 28 per cent the chair and the head wrote it jointly, while in 22 per cent of schools it was the head alone who wrote the first draft of the governors' report.

What do they say?

The NFER group analysed the contents of some 200 reports and found that most kept to the minimum requirements of the DES Circular 8/86. Many of them appeared to be little more than lists, though some invited comment on particular issues at the annual meeting.

How do they say it?

The NAGM members stressed that the style should be clear, concise and jargon free. However, the NFER group found that the 200 or so reports which they studied were characterised by so much jargon that they appeared to have been written '. . . by educationists for educationists', though primary schools generally were rather better than secondary schools at using straightforward language. Few schools seem to have produced their reports in any language other than English – only one out of Buglione's 51 ILEA schools, for instance.

The overall verdict of the NFER group indicates just how much room there is for improvement:

> . . . it is probably true to say that about 10 per cent of the governors' reports analysed would have interested parents, had they arrived on their doormat or in their child's pocket.
>
> (Earley, 1988, p.7)

How then can governors improve their annual reports to parents so that the reports actually fulfil their potential for promoting the partnership between parents, governors and the school?

Ways to Improve Governors' Annual Reports

- Use a representative group of governors to write the first draft with the assistance of the head.
- Write in a friendly, informal and straightforward style without jargon.
- Explain any technical terms or acronyms which you cannot avoid using.
- Put unavoidable lists in appendices at the back, e.g. National Curriculum test results.
- Use a question and answer approach to make the report accessible to all, e.g. 'Who are the governors?' 'Who do they represent?' 'Where does the money come from?' 'Where does it go?'
- Use questions to signal topics suitable for discussion at the annual meeting, e.g. 'Should we spend more money on musical instruments?' 'Would you like your child to receive sex education at school?'
- Use children's pictures to make the report more attractive.
- Use a word processor and a photocopier to produce an easy-to-read document that does not give parents the wrong idea about how much money the school has in its budget!

---

iv The annual parents' meeting

Section 31 of the Education (No.2) Act 1986 requires governors to hold an annual meeting for all the parents of children at the school.

The meeting allows for discussion of the annual report and of how the governors, head and LEA have carried out their duties concerning the school. If the number of parents present is equivalent to at least 20 per cent of the number of pupils on roll then the meeting may pass a resolution on any matter which relates to those topics. A resolution must be considered by the governors and copies sent to the head and the LEA if it is relevant to them. They, in turn, must consider the resolution and comment in writing in time for their comments to be included in the next annual governors' report.

There is here a clear analogy with the board of directors of a company holding an annual meeting of shareholders to account for the use they have made of the shareholders' money. For the first time in the history of school government, governors are being held accountable to the parents for their effectiveness in governing the school.

Not surprisingly, the prospect of such meetings aroused feelings of anxiety in many governors and headteachers. In the event their anxiety was unfounded, since the great majority of annual parents' meetings were characterised more by apathy than antipathy. The NFER conference report (Earley, 1988), referred to above in connection with governors' reports, contains somewhat depressing evidence about the first round of annual meetings. However, amongst the factual evidence of parental apathy towards a formal governors' meeting one can find clear pointers to ways of using this meeting to promote parental involvement in the school.

Who came?

Circular 8/86 suggested that – in addition to the governors, the head and the parents, who all have a right to attend – it would be worth considering inviting some members of the teaching and non-teaching staff and a representative of the LEA. It was, in the view of the DES, '... unlikely to be desirable to invite the press or members of the public'. An invitation to attend does not entitle a person to vote. Only parents may vote.

According to the NFER School Governors Research Group's national survey, the number of governors attending the annual parents' meeting varied widely. Buglione in ILEA Division 9 found a marked variation between county and voluntary primary schools. In county primary schools the average governor attendance was 57 per cent whereas for voluntary schools the figure was 72 per cent. It seems reasonable to surmise that parents are likely to doubt the commitment of a governing body if nearly half of the governors fail to turn up for their own meeting.

If average attendance rates for governors are disappointing then those for parents are dismal. All the studies confirm the picture gathered from many heads at the time: the number of parents attending varied widely but was generally very low. Note that figures for parental attendance are given as a percentage of the number of pupils on roll rather than of the number of parents eligible to attend, because the precise number of eligible parents was difficult to determine before the introduction of the register of parents. The NFER group found attendances varying from 0 per cent to 169 per cent of pupils on roll, with an overall average of just under 5 per cent. Generally the smaller the school the higher the attendance. Bristow's national survey found the same average of 5 per cent. In London Buglione found a higher overall average of 9.5 per cent but noted a significant difference between county primary schools at 7.5 per cent and voluntary schools at 15 per cent. This is an interesting replication of the figures for governor attendance and raises the question of what underlies the parallel between governor and parent attendance. Does one cause the other? If so, which way round? Or are they both symptoms of something else about the school in general? The NFER group quote an LEA observation on how governors and heads explained their attendance figures:

> Those disappointed with the low turnout consoled themselves with the inference that this must represent a high level of satisfaction among the parent community. Conversely those few schools with a high turnout regarded this as evidence of strong parental support!
>
> (Earley, 1988, p.8)

From a head's point of view however, such public displays of apparent lack of interest in the school undermine their efforts in other ways to build close relationships with the parents and the rest of the community. They also signify a lost opportunity to extend this work in a new way which would help governors feel that their role is both real and potentially rewarding. For these reasons it is important for heads to help their governing bodies to achieve a high turnout of parents for the annual meeting.

What did they talk about?

The NFER group found that most meetings started with an introduction by the chair of the governors, moved on to a consideration of the annual report, and then took questions from the floor on other topics; discussion was largely harmonious but stilted. The meetings were usually held in the school hall with the governors and the head facing the parents, and lasted for an average of one hour. In Bristow's survey 87 per cent of the meetings dealt exclusively with the annual report and lasted an average of 77 minutes. The vast majority of meetings were not quorate and so could not pass formal resolutions, but even those that were rarely actually passed a resolution. Discussion seems to have been wide-ranging but mostly harmonious. Buglione produced a list in rank order of topics discussed but these may well reflect the rather different concerns of parents in the metropolis. The top four were: staff shortages and cover for absent staff; sex education and child abuse; the police in school policy; the teachers' industrial action.

Bristow asked the chairs of governors in his survey whether they considered the meeting to have been a success. A majority did consider the meeting successful though this figure rose where the meeting had been combined with some other event, 70 per cent as against 53 per cent. It is worth noting that he also found that combined meetings were better attended and lasted longer. Ormston found that the meetings that were lively became:

> . . . a celebration of the success of the schools to which governors and parents were committed.
>
> (Earley, 1988, p.35)

This raises the question of how heads can help governors make the most of the annual parents' meeting in order that a genuine partnership between school, governors and parents may be developed.

Making the Most of Annual Parents' Meetings

A. Improving Attendance

- Link with another event which is already attractive to parents, e.g. concert, video of school trip, exhibition of children's work.
- Suggest in the annual report that parents' views will be sought on some unresolved issues, e.g. uniform, educational visits, sex education.
- Provide creche or child-minding facilities.
- Invite parents to the meeting in a friendly letter rather than just as part of the annual report.
- Give good notice of the meeting and then send reminders including one on the day itself.

- Arrange interpreters for non-English speaking parents, and interpreters and signers for deaf parents, if appropriate, and then make sure parents know these facilities will be available.
- Hold the meeting at the end of the spring term – the new pupils will have settled in and the summer term is already overloaded with events in most primary schools.

B. Improving the Meeting

- Start with the refreshments, it breaks the ice and encourages the less confident to join in when the meeting is under way.
- Wear names – especially the governors and staff, but the parents too, if possible (sticky address labels are cheap and don't damage clothing). Remember the only thing linking everyone at the meeting is the school, most people will know only a few of the others.
- Make big, clear name cards to place in front of each governor during the meeting itself – many parents complain that they have no idea who these people are.
- Avoid using too big a room. It is much better to have to move to a bigger room because so many people have turned up (it creates an atmosphere of success) than to have a disappointing handful in the hall.
- Use adult-sized chairs – child-sized chairs make parents feel uncomfortable, irritable and impatient.
- Arrange the chairs in a horseshoe or circle – the meeting is intended to be cooperative not confrontational.
- Chair should introduce him/herself, provide any update to the annual report and get the meeting under way – avoid reading out the report, which is repetitious and boring.
- Involve the other governors by getting each to deal with a particular topic or area of interest.
- Get the clerk to keep notes on a flipchart so that everyone can see what has been said; the notes will also provide a useful focus for the governors' discussion at their next meeting.
- Defuse any antagonism by offering to arrange a private meeting with the head or LEA.
- If the discussion gets bogged down by a tenacious parent, ask the meeting if it wants to move on to the next item.
- Tell the meeting that you will respond as soon as possible in the school newsletter to any issues raised at the meeting – a year is too long to wait for a response.

- Consider dividing the parents into workshop style groups for discussion purposes if you have attracted a good attendance.
- Persuade your LEA that governors need training in running meetings and in presentational skills.
- End on a positive note, praising the successes of the past year – it is easy for people to go away with an intangible, disgruntled feeling from such meetings.

---

v The employment of staff

The position of the governing body regarding the employment of teaching and non-teaching staff depends on the status of the school. The position of grant maintained schools and schools with delegated budgets is covered by the Education Act 1988. County and voluntary schools with non-delegated budgets are subject to the provisions of the Education (No.2) Act 1986.

Prior to the implementation of the 1986 Act, the LEA (although practice varied from authority to authority) was the dominant partner in all matters of the employment of staff in respect of county and voluntary controlled primary schools. In voluntary aided schools, and in respect of the reserved teacher in voluntary controlled or special agreement schools, the governors have always held the greater power. The fine detail of procedures for appointment and dismissal of staff need not concern us here: this may be found in the articles of government for each school. What is important is the principle. The two Acts both increase the power of the governors at the expense of the LEA. They differ in the degree to which they do this.

The 1986 Act gives the LEA the power to decide whether a teaching appointment should be made. Once that decision has been taken, the power of selection passes to the governing body, who make their choice of candidate and recommend that the appointment be made. The LEA has a right to participate in the selection procedure and may decline to appoint the person of the governors' choice if it can show good cause. A similar principle applies to non-teaching appointments. For headteacher appointments a panel composed equally of governors and LEA nominees undertakes the selection process, with the LEA retaining a final right of veto. In the matter of dismissals, the LEA remains the dominant partner though it is required to consult the head and the governors. For schools that are covered by the provisions of the 1986 Act, the governors are effectively the selectors of teaching and non-teaching staff but the power to dismiss rests with the LEA.

The 1988 Act gives much greater power to the governors of grant maintained schools and of schools with delegated budgets.

Grant maintained schools

Grant maintained schools are effectively completely independent of the LEA which formerly maintained them and are governed by their own articles of government.

Maintained schools with delegated budgets

Of more interest is the position of maintained schools with delegated budgets. The governing body of such a school has the power to determine, within its budget and subject to its duty to deliver the National Curriculum, how many staff will work at the school. The governors select their own candidate for appointment to a teaching post. While it has a duty to consider any advice the Chief Education Officer may offer, the LEA must appoint the candidate selected by the governors unless that person is disqualified on grounds of qualifications, health, physical capacity or misconduct. A similar situation applies in the case of non-teaching appointments, subject to a requirement to consult the CEO if the appointment is for 16 hours or more per week. The power to appoint headteachers and deputies is similarly largely in the hands of the governing body. In these cases the CEO has a right to attend and to give advice which the governors have a duty to 'consider', but the selection panel is set up by the governing body and does not include any LEA nominees. The power to dismiss rests effectively with the governors. The CEO and the head both have a right to attend but the LEA must dismiss an employee if the governors so recommend after following due procedures. Additionally, the LEA must accept the costs of a dismissal, only charging the school in exceptional circumstances.

Voluntary aided schools with delegated budgets are in almost the same position as other schools. The already extensive autonomy of governing bodies of such schools is strengthened by the removal of the LEA's right to set a complement of staff, to veto teaching appointments and to prevent dismissals.

These powers, which were little discussed during the passage of the bill largely because they were part of the section covering delegated budgets, represent a very great increase in the power and responsibilities of governors; the power of the LEA is reduced to that of a rubber stamp in all matters of employment in the delegated budget schools which they maintain and for which they remain ultimately accountable to the electorate. If governors are going to exercise these considerable powers in such a way that the effectiveness of the school is enhanced, then they will have very definite training needs. The paramount need for a close, trusting and open relationship with the head teacher is also evident.

vi Managing the school's budget

The employment situation in schools with delegated budgets discussed above is, of course, just one aspect of the responsibilities placed upon governors as a result of local financial management. While governors will retain oversight of this aspect of the management of the school, the major responsibilities are delegated to the head. This topic is discussed in detail in Chapter Eight so at this point I just wish to signal that this is another area in which the governors' powers have been extended at the expense of the LEA, and that consequently the importance of the relationship between the head and the governing body is greatly enhanced.

vii The head's report

Section 32 of the Education (No.2) Act 1986 requires heads to make such reports to the governing body as that body may request. That the requirement should be statutory may have been new but the head's report has long been the centrepiece of the governors' termly meeting.

The problem for the head is one of judging how much information to include on how many topics. Here it is a question of striking the right balance, of providing enough to allow the governors to understand an issue without saturating them with only marginally relevant information. It is easy for a head who knows the topic in detail to overload, and thus bore, governors. The governors are, after all, volunteers using their leisure time in the interests of the community. A number of the new heads in Weindling and Earley's (1987) study were disappointed with the level of involvement of their governors but this may have been the result of 'unrealistic' expectations by the heads of a group of volunteers. More realistic perhaps was the remark of one head concerning his report to the governors:

> You need to keep the governors fully informed, but you don't want to bore the pants off them!
>
> (Quoted by Weindling and Earley, 1987, p.157)

On the other hand, in the past many heads undoubtedly erred in providing too little information to their governing bodies. Many new heads use their predecessor's reports as a rough model when writing their first report to governors, but in times of rapid and extensive change in the responsibilities of governors this is even less likely to prove satisfactory. Furthermore, even experienced heads need to reconsider their reports in the light of these changes.

It is neither possible nor desirable to give a definitive list of those matters which should be included in the head's report. Schools differ, governing bodies differ and the issues faced by schools change over time. These are, however, some guiding principles and some areas where governors have a clear right to be kept informed by the head. Some LEAs issue guidelines to heads indicating those areas which should be covered by their reports, but even in such authorities Kogan *et al.* (1984) noted wide variation between schools. That variation in content may be fully justified by the differences between schools themselves. What is less easily justified is the variation in style. Some heads in Kogan's study were factual in their reporting while others were openly polemical, putting only their view of an issue. Some governors receiving a partisan report may not be in a position to see that there are other views, even within the school, on a particular issue and that there are therefore different options which are not being put before them. While it is probably inevitable that heads will to some degree present issues in the light of their particular view of the world, a more neutral, factual approach is more appropriate to a written report.

Organisation of Headteacher's Report

ILEA suggested a long list of topics which should be included in the headteacher's report to the governors. The topics were organised into six categories and those categories might well be useful to a head in any LEA as a basis for organising the report:

1. The children, their parents and the community.
e.g. roll; attendance; minority groups; free meals; suspensions; parent/community links.

2. Teaching organisation; school staff; responsibility structure; staff development; ancillary staff.
e.g. organisation of classes; any special arrangements; pupil

teacher ratio (PTR); responsibilities of staff; staff changes; staff development programme.

3. The curriculum.
e.g. new initiatives; meeting children's individual needs; guidelines; record keeping; extra-curricular activities.

4. Organisation and management.
e.g. consultation and communication procedures with staff; resources.

5. The building.
e.g. amenities; difficulties; work planned; work carried out.

6. The future.
e.g. proposed future developments; school development plan.

Source: ILEA Circular 82/95, Appendix A

viii Admissions

No date has yet been set for the implementation of the 'open enrolment' provisions of the 1988 Act in primary schools. This Act increases governors' powers over admissions marginally but, until these are made effective for primary schools, admissions continue to be regulated by the Education Act 1980, which places responsibility for admissions, subject to certain statutory provisions, upon the LEA in respect of county and voluntary controlled schools. Parents who are dissatisfied with the LEA's decision may appeal to an independent appeal committee whose decision is binding upon the LEA and the governors.

ix Grant maintained status

The ultimate power which school governing bodies possess is that of initiating a change of status which takes the school completely outside LEA control. Views differ about how many governing bodies will see grant maintained status as the answer to their problems, with even the Prime Minister and the Secretary of State failing to agree on that topic. However, what is beyond all doubt is that the very existence of this provision will ensure that the balance of power between the LEA and the governing body will be firmly in the governors' favour. Thus 'opting out' is the weapon of last resort, the ultimate deterrent, the nuclear bomb of school government.

The right-wing think tank, the Centre for Policy Studies (CPS), which has had such an influence on government education policy, describes opting out as an attack on the 'monopoly of local authority-delivered education'. They claim that state education will be strengthened by providing better quality and greater choice for parents and more freedom for heads and governors:

> If the local authority hinders heads and governors from running their schools as they wish, and if it fails to provide parents with the education and schools they want . . . then schools will choose to be rid of their shackles.
>
> (Lawlor, 1988, p.6)

In view of the awesome responsibilities that governors will be taking on if they take the school out of LEA control, it seems unlikely that many governing bodies will choose to initiate a change to grant maintained status unless there are particularly compelling reasons. The mere existence of the right to opt out will in most cases have proved sufficient to have tipped the balance of power decisively towards the governing body.

Should a governing body decide to go ahead with opting out of LEA control they still have to secure the support of the parents as expressed through a secret ballot. A simple majority of votes is sufficient for the proposal to go forward provided that at least 50 per cent of the parents have voted. If the number of votes is lower than 50 per cent then another ballot must be held, and that result is binding however few parents vote. It is difficult to predict how popular a change of status will prove to parents. It seems likely that the attitude of the head will be a major influence on parents' views as on those of governors.

The workings of governing bodies

The recent government initiatives in school government see the governing body as a way of achieving accountability. The governors' job is to ensure that the school is working effectively for the community it serves. An additional function of the governing body is to provide a forum in which various interest groups are represented. The clearest manifestation of this function is in the composition of the governing body where parents, staff, LEA and local commercial and industrial interests all have their representatives. Kogan (1984) found that quite a different model was favoured by headteachers in the early 1980s, that of the 'supportive' governing body which championed the school. While there may still be an element of the 'Supporters' Club' in the new governing bodies, that can no longer be seen as their prime function.

The majority of governing bodies, according to Kogan, operated in what he called a 'spasmodic' mode. These bodies came to life only for their termly meeting. Between meetings only the chairman was likely to have any continuing involvement with the school as a governor. Governing bodies will find it hard to discharge their new responsibilities with such an intermittent way of working. They will need to adopt Kogan's 'continuous' mode of work, whereby they hold more meetings to examine particular issues; use sub-committees or working parties for certain areas like finance, staffing or curriculum; and have a continuing programme of visits to the school to ensure that they have the necessary knowlege to make their decisions. The spasmodic mode fitted well with a chairman who used a 'single-handed' style and, together with the head, dealt with everything that cropped up between meetings. His observations led him to conclude that:

> The realities of power, in school governing bodies, circle at present around the headteacher and the chairman.
>
> (Kogan, 1984, p.179)

The new situation needs a chairman who uses what Kogan called a 'consensual' style, working with the governing body as a collective, ensuring that every governor is involved. In practice, Kogan found that governing bodies operated in their meetings like a series of concentric circles. At the centre lay the chairman and the head who ran the meeting; in the next ring lay a group of governors who occasionally contributed to the proceedings; while beyond them lay another ring whose participation '. . . took the form of nods of agreement'. His description has the ring of truth to anyone who has attended a number of governors' meetings.

Kogan found a connection between the head's leadership style and the way in which the governing body functioned. The autocratic head tended to relate only to the chairman, with the rest of the governing body having little involvement in decision making. Even democratic heads could sideline the governing body by emphasising the internal nature of policy making. The governing body here were informed of the result of the process in which the professional teachers had participated, and were expected merely to legitimise it. What seems to be called for by the new situation, in which governing bodies have extensive and more clearly defined duties and responsibilities, is a democratic style of headship which involves the governors in the decision making process.

Conclusion

Exactly one hundred years after the Cross Commission Report endorsed the system of school managers, the DES has been advertising for governors to fulfil the demanding role which the 1986 and 1988 Acts have created. This advertisment from the *Radio Times* succinctly summarises that role and calls for a set of qualities strikingly similar to those identified by the Cross Report:

Do you care about your child's education?

Do you feel you have no say in important decisions about your child's education? Do you wish you had the opportunity to make your views known? You should think about becoming a school governor.

All sorts of people can be school governors; parents, businessmen and women, people from the local community, as well as teachers from the school and people appointed by the local authority. There aren't any special qualifications – unless you count common sense, an interest in education and the ability to spare some time for meetings and visits.

Your job will be to help decide what is taught, to help select teachers, to help decide how the school's budget is spent and to set overall standards of behaviour. It's a challenging, interesting role.

Find out about being a school governor by contacting your local school or local education authority.

Shouldn't you become a school governor?

Source: DES advertisement in *Radio Times* 20.8.88

We must all hope that people of the right quality, who are motivated by altruism and a sense of community service, respond to such calls. The recent changes have made the role of school governor more powerful than at any time since the establishment of state education, and that increased power means that the relationship between the head and the governing body is of pivotal importance.

Further reading

The impact of the Education Reform Act 1988 is so substantial upon school governing bodies that it has outdated all of the current handbooks. However new editions are likely to appear in some quantity. One book of continuing relevance is:

Kogan, M. *et al.* (1984) *School Governing Bodies*. London: Heinemann. This book provides an illuminating discussion of the issues involved in school government, based upon a three-year research project on the workings of governing bodies.

CHAPTER 2

Relationships with Parents

Every newly-appointed head will have had a greater or lesser degree of contact with parents when a class teacher, but this contact will most likely have been on an individual, ad hoc basis. The responsibility of the headteacher is for the policy of the whole school concerning relationships with parents. This is an area of school management where practice has changed substantially and those changes have, for the most part, been underpinned by research findings which demonstrate the importance of the relationship between home and school as one of the factors affecting pupils' achievement.

Most primary schools encourage parents to approach their child's class teacher with information about their child which they feel might affect the child in school. The class teacher is also the first point of contact for parents who are worried about some aspects of their child's behaviour or performance at school. Additionally, most schools arrange more formal meetings between parents and teachers. Typically these would consist of a 'Meet the Teacher' evening at the beginning of the school year, when parents have a chance to meet the child's new teacher and pass on any information which they think the teacher ought to know. Towards the end of the year, often following a written report on the child's progress, an 'Open Evening' provides parents with an opportunity to see something of their child's work and the chance to discuss their child's progress with the teacher. Many schools now go considerably further than this in their arrangements for parental contact, and the class teacher may have parent helpers in the classroom or on visits.

Practice differs significantly from school to school and considerable variation may even be found from class to class within a school. This internal variation arises most frequently from a view that such decisions should be left to the individual teacher who, acting as a professional, will make his or her decision in the light of what he/she perceives as the children's best interests. Such a policy leads to an inconsistency in practice which parents rightly find puzzling. The relationship with parents is so crucial that this is an area where the head needs to build a consensus amongst the staff and ensure that a school-wide policy operates.

For the head, the relationship with parents will differ in certain important respects. Firstly, the head is responsible for the school's policy on all aspects of parental involvement. Secondly, the head has more contacts with parents as a group. Thirdly, when meeting individual parents the nature of the interaction will be altered by the fact that the head is not normally the child's class teacher.

The head's responsibility for the whole school policy on parental involvement necessitates him or her being able to explain and justify that policy. This does not necessarily imply that such issues of policy should be the result of lone decision-making. On the contrary, the effective head is more likely to have ensured the full participation of the teaching staff in the process of making the decision. The policy should also have been discussed with the parent governors in particular and the governing body in general. Where a mechanism exists for discussing the proposed arrangements with the parents as a body, such as a PTA or other support group, then it would seem obvious that any such opportunity should be taken for consulting those most affected by the school's policy. In the absence of such a formal arena, other ways could be found of discovering the preferences of the parents. This might involve the calling of a special meeting or the distribution of a questionnaire. It is a truism, but one worth repeating, that people are more likely to be satisfied with arrangements that they have had a chance to shape.

Why promote parental involvement?

Amid all the issues competing for the head's attention, why should a policy on parental involvement be so high on the list of priorities? There are two answers reflecting the two strands of developments in this field. Firstly, the environment in which schools operate is one that sees participation as a legitimate parental right. Secondly, the evidence, unusually for research evidence, is unequivocal: effective schools involve parents as partners in the education process.

It is not necessary to recount the chain of events in the mid 1970s

(Tyndale, Ruskin, The Great Debate, Taylor Report) which led to the call for greater accountability on the part of schools. This development was matched by a parallel rise in 'consumerism' in many other spheres. Participation and accountability are most often portrayed as ways of making schools more responsive to the views of parents and the needs of society. Conspiracy theorists tend to view participation as a way both of making government more acceptable to the governed and of diverting attention from successive governments' failure to deliver successful economic policies. Either way, only a Canute would ignore the need to give account of the school to the parents.

The rationale for parents as partners in the process of educating their children has its origin principally in post-war research findings, most notably those of Douglas (1964) and Plowden (CACE, 1967). Douglas's longitudinal cohort study of every child in Britain born in one week in March 1946 found that achievement at ages eight and eleven correlated most closely with the level of parental interest. While parental interest also correlated with social class, he found that, within each class, children of interested parents scored more highly in achievement tests. He measured parental interest by means of ratings by teachers and the number of visits made to the school to discuss the child's progress. The survey commissioned by the Plowden Committee also found parental interest to be the strongest factor associated with achievement in school. The conclusion was irresistible, in the words of the Plowden Report:

> . . . a strengthening of parental encouragement may produce better performance in school.
>
> (CACE, 1967)

In the aftermath of the Plowden Report, primary schools were urged to find ways of increasing parents' involvement in the education of their children, with a view to increasing parents' understanding of what the school was trying to do. This heightened awareness would lead in its turn to more positive attitudes towards school and higher attainment on the part of the children.

The promotion of parental involvement has been a recurrent theme in the literature since the Plowden Report. The HMI Primary Education Survey (DES, 1978), for example, found that the percentage of classes receiving voluntary parental help fell as the age of the children rose. Thus 31 per cent of seven year-old classes received parental help whereas only 17 per cent of eleven year-old classes involved parents in this way. Most of this help consisted of assistance with children's welfare and with the supervision of children on educational visits (DES, 1978, p.35). The Inspectorate pointed out that, paradoxically, while the public at large had become less satisfied with school in general:

> . . . the relations between teachers and individual parents have become closer and more friendly.
>
> (DES, 1978, p.126)

Improving Primary Schools (ILEA, 1985), widely known as the Thomas Report after its chairman Norman Thomas, contains a whole chapter devoted to the topic. The Committee made a point of meeting groups of parents at most of the seventy-six schools they visited. The report mentions the presence of parents working as volunteers in schools as one of the 'most obvious changes in primary education over the last two decades' (ILEA, 1985, p.84). The Committee observed parents helping prepare resources, translating materials into the various languages used at home, mounting and displaying children's work, talking about their jobs, accompanying visits and hearing reading. While recognising the need for caution in developing parental involvement, the Committee was clearly in favour of increased involvement of this type:

> To deny the opportunity of being helped seems a curious act of self-denial.
>
> (ILEA, 1985, p.85)

The Junior School Project (ILEA, 1986) followed some two thousand pupils through junior school, measuring the children's performance and looking for correlations with features of the children's background, school policies and teachers' practices. The team, led by Peter Mortimore, identified twelve 'key factors of effectiveness' which lay within the control of the head and teachers. Parental involvement is to be found on the list:

> The research found parental involvement to be a positive influence upon pupils' progress and development. This included help in classrooms and on educational visits, and attendance at meetings to discuss children's progress. The headteacher's accessibility to parents was also important, showing that schools with an informal, open-door policy were more effective. Parental involvement in pupils' educational development within the home was also beneficial. Parents who read to their children, heard them read, and provided them with access to books at home, had a positive effect upon their children's learning.
>
> (ILEA, 1986, p.37)

Ways of promoting parental involvement

1. The school brochure

The Education Act 1980 made this a statutory requirement for maintained schools. However the information which is required statutorily is very basic and, given that the school has to produce a brochure, it would seem wise to extend the information about the school and its activities beyond the minimum required. The brochure will be, for many parents, crucial in terms of their image of the school. The care taken in its preparation and production is indicative of the school's attitude to its clientele.

Any school would do well to look at its current brochure and assess how far it achieves the four functions discerned by a group of teachers working with tutors from Nottingham University when they studied a wide range of written communications between school and home:

1) Basic Information Model: makes necessary information available; concern for organizational efficiency.
2) Development Model: provides information and support during the process of entry/transfer.
3) Public Relations Model: projects a positive image of the life and work of the school.
4) Parental Involvement Model: encourages parents to become actively involved in the education of their children and in the life and work of the school.

(Bastiani, 1978, p.9)

In view of the fact that the brochure is intended to remain a source of useful information for parents for a period of time, it would seem to be wise to involve parents in its preparation. A PTA might well be able to give helpful advice about what information parents would like included and the manner of its presentation. Indeed, a study funded by the Scottish Consumers Council (Atherton, 1982) of the handbooks issued for parents by schools in Scotland, included this as one of its recommendations:

> Parents and their representatives should play a key role in the preparation of handbooks intended for their own use. They should be consulted about the information to be included in the handbook and be encouraged to provide any editorial and other assistance in the production of the handbook.

(Atherton, 1982, p.94)

Where the school serves a multi-lingual catchment area the brochure should be available in the principal languages used by the parents. The translation of the brochure need not be costly if community links are used, and its provision can say much more to a minority group about the schools' attitude towards them than any internal policy statement, however noble in intention.

2. *Starting school*

First impressions formed by new parents and their children may prove surprisingly durable. It it therefore important that time be given to meeting new parents, whether as a group when their children enter together or individually when they transfer from another school. When children are starting school for the first time the most effective arrangement seems to be for the children to spend time in the school, meeting the kind of activity they will encounter when they actually start. This type of visit also enables the parents to meet the head, see and hear something of the school's activities, and have their questions answered and fears allayed.

3. *Newsletters*

The regular production of a newsletter giving information on, say, a monthly basis is a feature of many schools' communications with the parents. This is a convenient way of avoiding the production of a plethora of 'notes' and has the added advantage of informing parents of activities in all the classes rather than just the one attended by their child. While these newsletters need not be glossy, it is surprisingly easy to produce attractive printed material using a photocopier and a pair of scissors. As with the brochure, the care taken says much about the school's attitude. Even more important than the newsletter's physical appearance is the tone of the language used. It is only too easy to appear to 'talk down' or to present a 'take it or leave it' attitude to parents. In their conclusions the group of teachers from Nottingham stressed that the language used revealed the values and prejudices of the writers:

> Throughout the range of written forms of contact schools reveal a great deal of themselves, often more than they realise and sometimes more than they mean to!
>
> (Bastiani, 1978, p.114)

Some of the more obvious traps for the unwary writer can be avoided by asking a non-teacher colleague, say the school secretary, to read through the final draft. Such a reading can reveal ambiguities in the wording as well as provide a reaction to the tone used by the writer.

4. Parents as helpers in school

The use of parents as unpaid helpers in the school, in the classroom and on educational visits is now so widespread that it would probably be difficult to find a primary school which did not use its parents in this way. The forms of help which parents can offer seem unlimited: covering library books; coaching sports teams; putting up bookshelves; hearing children read; helping children with cooking and needlework; and talking to children about their hobbies and jobs.

It would be unrealistic to pretend that there are no problems associated with using parents in school; some may not be motivated solely by an altruistic desire to help. There seems also to be a more fundamental dilemma in that the opportunities offered to parents tend to be of a very menial nature and might be seen as reflecting a certain reluctance on the part of the teachers to admit parents to anything approaching a participatory role. There is also a danger that the school creates an 'in group' and an 'out group', so that those parents who are either not asked to help or are simply not available to help feel excluded from the cosy band of helpers.

5. Parents as teachers of their own children

One of the most exciting developments in the field of parental involvement concerns parents hearing their own children read at home.

Research undertaken in Dagenham (Hewison and Tizard, 1980), which involved interviewing parents in their homes, seemed to show that whether the parents heard their children read at home was a very important factor in the child's progress at primary school. The Haringey Reading Project established, under experimental conditions, that randomly selected groups of children whose parents heard them read achieved higher scores in reading tests than children whose parents did not hear them read at home. Somewhat surprisingly, the parents doing the hearing were in some cases themselves illiterate while others were literate only in languages other than English.

These results have led to a number of schools establishing schemes of their own. Perhaps the best known is the one originated in Hackney: Parents and Children and Teachers (PACT). This scheme involves the parents in hearing their child read two or three times a week at home from a book brought home from school. A card is used to keep a record of the pages heard, and parents are encouraged to write comments on the card to which the teacher replies: thus a dialogue is established between the parent and the teacher. The early signs from these schemes are of substantial increases in children's reading scores. Some of the participants also claim more wide-ranging benefits in terms of increased mutual understanding between home and school. Some schools, notably in Hackney, have introduced similar schemes which extend home teaching by parents to mathematics. It remains to be seen whether maths is equally susceptible of being taught in this way.

6. *The Parent Teacher Association*

PTAs, and less formal versions like 'Friends of the School', are now considerably more widespread than when the Plowden Committee reported in 1967. Most PTAs are primarily fund-raising organisations and relieve the school staff of what many teachers perceive as a time-consuming chore which, in an ideal world, they ought not to have to undertake. Given the ever-rising requirements of primary schools for expensive equipment like computers and photocopiers, and given also the restrictive financial climate, it is scarcely surprising that the number of PTAs has risen in recent years. What is more surprising perhaps is the recent finding by the ILEA *Junior School Project* that the existence of a PTA has no effect either way on the progress and performance of junior age pupils. (ILEA, 1986, p.37).

Quite why this should be is not clear. It could be, as Mortimore suggests (*ibid*, p.38) that the formal aspect of the organisation is not likely to encourage a wide membership of the PTA by all social groups amongst the parents. Or it might be simply an indication of how many schools are missing the opportunity to use the PTA as another means of facilitating communication both ways between home and school.

7. *Parents' annual meeting*

Section 31 of the Education (No.2) Act 1986 requires the governors of all schools to hold an annual meeting of the parents. The function of this meeting is to discuss the governors' report and the way in which the head, the LEA and the governors have discharged '. . . their functions in relation to the school'. (Section 31, 2a). It may be that the formal nature of this meeting will inhibit many parents from attending and playing a full part. However, the fact that the meeting is a statutory requirement does not mean that the meeting itself need be formal in terms of its atmosphere. Provided that the school can attract a large and representative number of parents to the meeting this could prove to be an invaluable means of allowing parents an effective voice in the formation of school policy. Past experience suggests that almost every parent will attend school if the focus of attention is their own child, as it is at an Open Evening. To persuade the great majority that the parents' meeting is equally important will require greater ingenuity and a clear understanding that the consultation and discussion is not a mere sham. In view of the fact that the parents' meeting has the power to pass resolutions which must be considered by the governors and, if necessary, the head and the LEA, then a head who approaches the parents' meeting without an evident willingness to consider the views of the parents is likely to find him/herself in considerable difficulties at some point in the future.

The message concerning parental involvement in all its many aspects is clear: we have moved out of the era, if it ever truly existed, when parents were happy to leave all the decisions concerning their children's education to the school. Schools which have moved wholeheartedly into a partnership with parents in the joint enterprise of educating their children are, as a result, more effective in achieving their aims of promoting their pupils' progress and development.

Further reading

Griffiths, A. and Hamilton, D. (1984) *Parent, Teacher, Child*. London: Methuen. This book describes in detail how to establish and operate a 'PACT' scheme of parental involvement in their child's reading. Its style is clear and informative.

Tizard, B. *et al.* (1981) *Involving Parents in Nursery and Infant Schools*. London: Grant McIntyre. An invaluable book on parental involvement. Part I considers the issues and looks at the research findings which underpin the movement towards greater parental involvement. Part II contains a wealth of ideas and suggestions for how to go about increasing parental involvement. The style is especially clear and readable. The book is also highly relevant to primary schools which include juniors.

CHAPTER 3

Relationships with the Local Education Authority

Reading the press, one gets the impression that headteachers are constantly in dispute with their local education authority. The names of McGoldrick and Honeyford spring to mind to substantiate the view that the relationship is acrimonious and contentious. This view is far from an accurate picture of how the great majority of heads and of LEAs relate to each other.

For most heads, the relationship with the LEA which employs them is one of mutual cooperation marred only by the occasional wrangle over staffing, buildings and resources. Even at these times of disagreement, most heads do not lose sight of the fact that the individual officer with whom they are dealing is in the unenviable position of having to carry out a policy devised by others which is intended to control local government expenditure. Nor do the officers forget that in arguing for favourable treatment for their own schools heads are doing only that which they would expect them to do.

Weindling and Earley (1987) tell us that only 7 per cent of the new and 8 per cent of the old heads in their study had problems developing good relationships with LEA officers. From Mortimore's (1988) study of junior schools in the ILEA we find that the vast majority of the heads they interviewed were satisfied with the level of support they received from their local divisional office. This evidence clearly does not support the view that there is widespread unrest amongst heads about their relationship with the LEA.

In a sense it is not possible to have a relationship with a local education authority. Rather, the head has relationships with a variety of different people within an authority. The identity of the person varies according to the subject being dealt with. The range of subjects covers just about every aspect of school life: provision for children with special needs may involve contact with an educational psychologist and an officer responsible for that area; work on the school buildings may involve contact with a building surveyor from the architect's department; the employment of a caretaker may involve the personnel section. The particular arrangements vary from LEA to LEA in a way that makes it impossible to be specific. In most LEAs, however, there will be a particular officer and a particular adviser with whom the head deals.

The education officer

Most education officers are ex-secondary school teachers and heads of department. They are most unlikely to have had direct experience of either primary schools or of headship. The more senior ones will, however, have extensive experience of the education service and will have learned from dealing with the problems of schools and their headteachers over a number of years.

Few studies of officers exist and none of them are recent, so we do not know how far Rendell's (1968) and David's (1977) finding that most Chief Education Officers had Oxbridge arts degrees still applies. Nor do we know whether education officers today still lack the same skills as did those of 1977 who:

> . . . did not have special skills, except knowledge of education from being teachers and traditional administration.
>
> (David, 1977, p.202)

Hall *et al*. (1986) looked at four secondary headteachers at work and found that the amount of contact which heads had with the LEA varied greatly even within the same authority. They also noted that heads sometimes had a conflict of loyalty between that owed to the LEA and that owed to their own school. Although officers' attitudes varied, most valued regular telephone contact with heads in their area:

> You're looking for someone who will ring up, talk it through; not the arrogant bloke who thinks it's a sign of weakness to ring up an officer.
>
> (Officer quoted by Hall *et al*., 1976, p.198)

However good the working relationship with the officers, it is with the adviser or inspector that most heads will have their closest links with the authority.

The adviser or inspector

Many primary heads have only a vague idea of the role of the adviser or inspector. Stillman and Grant, who have conducted a major piece of research on the roles, management and practices of LEA advisory services, reported that teachers showed this vagueness and found that:

> . . . there was often a considerable mismatch between expectations and actuality.
>
> (Greig, 1986)

Nor is it unknown for LEA officers to speculate somewhat uncharitably about what advisers actually do. Interestingly, it seems that even would-be advisers share the general uncertainty about the advisory role:

> Indeed, few advisers seemed to have had any clear idea of what advisory work entailed when they applied for and accepted their first advisory appointment.
>
> (Bolam *et al.*, 1978)

This lack of clarity is due in part to the very considerable variation in practice between the 104 LEAs and even between individual advisers within an LEA. As an example of this inter-LEA variation, Stillman and Grant (1988) cite the claim by one authority that its advisers spend over 65 per cent of their time in classrooms during lesson time whereas several other authorities estimated that this activity occupied 10 per cent or less of their advisers' time.

Why are advisers important to the head?

From the head's point of view the relationship with the adviser can be of critical importance to both him and the school. This importance derives from several features of the adviser's position in the authority.

Firstly, in most authorities the adviser is the key link between the schools and the authority. Thus the adviser will carry back to the 'office', and on around the system, judgements which he has reached about the school, its staff and the head. As we shall see later, most advisers are involved in the selection and appointments procedures of their authority. This involvement in writing references, shortlisting and interviewing gives their judgements about the quality of the head a special significance. However, it is not only headteachers seeking further career advancement who will want the authority – i.e. the adviser – to view their performance favourably. It is clearly in the interests of all heads that their reputation and that of their schools should be high. Life as a head can be uncertain in even the best managed school. There are many crises, from school reorganisation to staff disciplinary procedures, when a high reputation with the authority may prove helpful.

Secondly, advisers control access to resources. In many authorities advisers have sums of money under their direct control to which heads may seek access in order to support, say, a curriculum development in the school. Other resources, too, may be under the adviser's control. Increasingly they are able to deploy advisory teachers in schools for certain purposes. The time and energy of a skilful advisory teacher can be an invaluable resource in supporting a teacher who is facing difficulties, or in providing help for some development in the school. An advisory teacher can be used to make Joyce and Showers' (1980) scheme of presentation, demonstration, practice, feedback and coaching (see Chapter 9) a reality when implementing a change in the school. Advisers also frequently control, or have a large say in, the distribution of in-service training facilities such as places on courses, supply cover and money. It seems certain that financial delegation to schools will reduce the scope for advisers to help larger schools in some of these ways; but advisers will no doubt continue to be of importance to smaller schools where their impact has always been, potentially at least, proportionately much greater.

Thirdly, important though these forms of sponsorship and patronage may be, there is another more fundamental sense in which the adviser may be of importance to the primary head. The adviser can often be the only trusted and respected fellow professional who knows the school, its staff and its circumstances, to whom the head can turn for impartial advice. Headship can be very isolating. New heads are particularly at risk, as the *Junior School Project* (Mortimore *et al.* 1988) found out:

> . . . the need for support for new headteachers follows from our data that show that new heads (less than two years in post) are generally associated with less effective schools. . . . They have to create their leadership role at the time when they are least familiar with the school. In some cases the deputy head is their only ally, yet this person may have been a competitor for the post. In other cases, the staff will resist change and hanker after the style of a former headteacher. **Support for the head during the initial period of their headship is vital** . . .
>
> Mortimore *et al.*, 1988 p.276 (my emphasis)

Of course, the need for professional support is not just limited to new heads: the adviser can be uniquely well placed to fulfil the role of professional friend to any head. Whether or not advisers are able to carry out this crucial aspect of their role will depend on various factors. Clearly their personal qualities will partly determine their capacity for establishing open and trusting relationships. Their past experience may also affect their capacity to empathise with a headteacher.

Who are the advisers?

The overwhelming majority of advisers are ex-teachers, though in Bolam *et al.*'s. (1978) survey 8 per cent had no teaching experience whatever. Generally this survey showed that most advisers:

- were men 73%
- were aged 41+ 75%
- had 6+ years teaching experience 80%
- had held a promoted post 76%
- had not been a head 80%
- had higher qualifications than teachers in general
- were more likely to be ex-secondary than ex-primary

Unfortunately the figures do not show how many of the 20 per cent of advisers who had held headships were ex-primary heads. My own experience would suggest that the majority of primary phase advisers have been primary heads, whereas the majority of specialist subject advisers have been secondary teachers, often ex-heads of department. The main reason for this is pay. Until recently, advisers' salary scales were identical to heads' salary scales. For the large majority of primary heads, with their smaller schools and correspondingly lower pay, a move into an adviser's post represents promotion and a consequent pay rise. For most secondary heads an adviser's post, other than that of Chief Adviser, would be graded lower than the average secondary headship and so would mean demotion and a drop in pay. It is interesting to consider that the relationship between secondary heads and their adviser tends to be quite different from that between the primary head and the adviser. In terms of status and pay, advisers are superior to primary heads, but for secondary heads the status relationship is the opposite. It would be interesting to know how far this difference in status is responsible for producing the different relationship.

Primary advisers for primary schools?

This brings us to a number of structural factors which can affect the capacity of the adviser to act as a respected source of advice to the head. LEAs vary greatly in the structure, scope, extent and role of their advisory services. Perhaps the most significant difference between advisory services from the primary head's point of view, in the light of the information about advisers' backgrounds, is whether one's local adviser has any experience of teaching in a primary school. A structure which gives all advisers a 'pastoral' responsibility for a group of schools will mean that it is very unlikely that the adviser with this special responsibility will have any direct experience of working in a primary school, let alone of actually running one.

Other structures – for example, some of the area team systems – can provide a specialist primary adviser with responsibility for the primary schools in the area. Her Majesty's Inspectorate have long relied on the principle that their inspectors do not need to have worked in a primary school in order to advise those that do. This view holds that an intelligent, sensitive, well-educated, fair-minded person can perform the role effectively. This is a view that appeals most strongly to those who feel that they are themselves intelligent, sensitive, well-educated and fair-minded. It is not a view which appeals to many primary heads. One of Winkley's respondents, an infant head, is more typical of the views of those on the receiving end of the advice proffered by the inexperienced:

> It is wrong for nursery and infant schools (for example) to have their principal source of advice from a general adviser whose background is – as it is for my school – exclusively as a secondary geography teacher.
> (Winkley, 1985, p.144)

Specialist primary phase advisers generally share this same view but their own numbers are so small in comparison with their ex-secondary colleagues that, in most authorities, they would be unable to provide a service to all of the primary schools.

An additional pressure of late has come in the form of a requirement in some authorities that all advisers should have some form of cross-phase responsibility. The rationale for this is the laudable one of reducing the discontinuity between phases. The effect, however, is to spread a scarce resource, specialist primary advisers, even more thinly. With the advent of the National Curriculum and the policing role of the advisory services, many LEAs are increasing the number of primary advisers which they employ. This may be good news for primary schools as long as the adviser's role does not become principally inspectorial.

Advisers as part of the LEA

LEAs also vary in terms of the relationship between the advisory service and the administrative service. Winkley (1985), in his illuminating study, develops a framework of three dimensions for classifying advisory services. He claims that advisory services differ in terms of:

(1) The degree of **integration** with the administration, e.g. Who leads the team? Do administrators have advisory responsibilities?
(2) The degree of **influence** which advisers have on the decision making process of the LEA, e.g. Do advisers have close contact with members? How much say do advisers have in the allocation of finances?
(3) The degree of **autonomy** from administrative direction, e.g. Does the advisory team determine its own priorities and way of working?

Winkley's framework was developed to assist his analysis of how advisory services function but it is useful to a practising head since it directs attention to three very significant aspects of any advisory service. Given the wide variation between LEAs, it is difficult to generate guidelines for heads who wish to develop a close relationship with their advisory service. The first step must be to find out about the advisory service in one's own LEA and Winkley has highlighted some of the more significant questions to ask.

What do advisers actually do?

As well as knowing about the structure of the advisory service and its relationship to the administration, one also needs to know about the content of its role – what do advisers actually do?

Stillman and Grant (1988) reported that while it was possible to draw up a list of advisers' tasks within a single LEA, the list would not necessarily apply to any other LEA. They also found a wide variation between individual advisers in a single LEA. Wilcox (1985), Chief Adviser at Sheffield, reflected upon the nature of the tasks that advisers are commonly required to carry out. He saw these tasks as falling into three broad categories: Evaluation; Change and Development; Systems Maintenance and Support. The table shows these three categories used as a framework to classify the major tasks of advisers which Bolam (1978) isolated. Winkley (1985) analysed forty job descriptions for advisers' jobs advertised during 1981/2. The table demonstrates strikingly the large number and varied nature of the tasks which comprise the Systems Maintenance and Support category. This is probably the part of the adviser's job about which people in

LEA Advisers' Activities

	EVALUATION	*CHANGE AND DEVELOPMENT*	*SYSTEMS MAINTENANCE AND SUPPORT*	
WILCOX, B. 'Clarifying the Role of the Adviser'. *Education*, 12/4/85, p.331.	Assessing standards and trends and providing information on the performance of the service. Data gathered by inspection and long term knowledge of the institution.	Moving the system forward in the light of changing priorities and needs. Use INSET; encourage involvement in innovative projects; foster and utilise research.	Advice, guidance and support given to the staff of education institutions, the LEA and other bodies. Attend governors' meetings, working parties, appointments, redeployments.	*Reflectively derived by Sheffield chief adviser.*
BOLAM, R. *et al.* (1978) *LEA Advisers and the Mechanism of Innovation*. Slough: NFER.	Evaluation and career development of individual staff. General inspection of a school or college.	Advising in a single institution (on major changes and developments). INSET LEA Wide Curriculum Change.	Staff appointments Advising individual staff about personal or professional matters. School visits (most frequent purpose). Advising on LEA wide structural and organisational changes.	*Empirically derived from questionnaires and interviews.*

	EVALUATION	*CHANGE AND DEVELOPMENT*	*SYSTEMS MAINTENANCE AND SUPPORT*	
[BOLAM, R. *et al.* continued]			Advising on the design, furnishing and equipping of schools. Advice to education committee. Advice on finances. Administrative and clerical work.	
WINKLEY, D. (1985) *Diplomats and Detectives*. London: Robert Royce.	Probationer Supervision (5) Inspection (7)	INSET (2) Curriculum Development (9) Project Development (12) Innovation (15)	Administration (1) Advising schools (2) Promotion of teachers (4) Building/Resources (6) Coordinating (8) Direction of centres etc. (13) Pastoral (14) Individual children (16) Legal/disciplinary (17)	*Derived from 40 job specifications – rank order of frequency in brackets.*

schools know least. The adviser's role in providing INSET or carrying out some form of inspection is much more visible to heads and teachers than is the time spent in committees, writing references, advising on financial procedures or being consulted about the design, furnishing and equipping of schools. Lack of knowledge about these aspects of the adviser's job probably accounts for a large part of the mismatch noted earlier between teachers' expectations and actuality.

The problem that remains, of course, is that the particular mix of these tasks which goes to make up any individual adviser's workload is still immensely variable.

To advise or to inspect?

One of the most significant areas of variation from the school point of view is the emphasis, or lack of it, on evaluation or more specifically on inspection. Even the title of the role varies, with some LEAs using the term 'adviser' while others use 'inspector'. However the title alone is not enough to indicate which function, inspectorial or advisory, is more prominent in any individual post. The title 'inspector' may denote a stress on the evaluative function, but it may instead have been chosen for rhetorical reasons to convey a tough managerial stance on the part of the authority.

At the time of Bolam's study in the early 1970s he noted that there was a general tendency to de-emphasise inspection in favour of advice and support. The William Tyndale case raised in stark form the role of the adviser in the area of quality control. How could the ILEA's inspectorate have been so incapable of preventing such an occurrence? This was one of the main questions to which the official ILEA inquiry directed its attention:

> The Authority's Inspectorate, in common with the inspectors of most other local education authorities, does not regard its prime function as being the inspection or checking of the quality of education being provided in the Authority's schools. The Inspectorate sees its main role as being the giving of advice and support to the teachers.
>
> (Auld, 1976, p.15)

In the wake of the Tyndale affair, ILEA greatly expanded the number of primary inspectors which it employed. Like LEAs throughout the country it also shifted the balance markedly towards the inspectorial function, as a result of more general moves towards tighter controls over schools in response to calls for increased accountability in education.

Thus, by the time that Walker (1981) was reporting the results of his research on advisers it was clear that:

> The move is generally to a more inspectorial role; in many LEAs general inspections of schools by LEA advisers are being introduced or reintroduced. . . their role [is] keeping a close watch and reporting on schools.
>
> (Walker, 1981, p.73)

The SSRC Cambridge Accountability Project came to the same conclusion:

> They are the 'quality control' agents of the LEA and, increasingly in the 1980s, are under pressure to develop their role as the eyes and ears of their Authority.
>
> (Elliott *et al.*, 1981, p.179)

Many advisers experience this tension between these two aspects of their role as difficult to resolve. Certainly most heads see it as something of a contradiction. It matters a great deal to the individual head whether the stress is on advising or inspecting.

In a case study which I carried out of one primary adviser and her relationships with a sample of the schools in her area, all of the heads, as well as the adviser herself, expressed strong views on this topic:

> 'The greatest strength is being able to admit mistakes to her – to be completely open, and I would feel less able to do that if she was called an inspector.' (Head C)
>
> 'It's almost a question of which side they're on.' (Head B)
>
> 'I wanted the role of colleague, confidante and adviser. . . An inspector is more evaluating – an agent of the LEA.' (Adviser)
>
> (Hill, 1985, pp 10–11)

Clearly the relationship is likely to be open and trusting if the emphasis is on advising rather than inspecting, though it would be simplistic to imagine that even the friendliest adviser is not at the same time making judgements about the head's performance. Furthermore, as a result of the adviser's position in the system, these are judgements which carry great weight and may be used as the basis for discussions which could affect both the head and his or her future and the school and its future.

The position of the adviser has been likened to that of Janus, facing both towards the school and also towards the 'office'. Walker (1981) sees them as occupying a gap between the administration and the schools. For some, this position can lead to a sense of isolation, a feeling that they truly belong to neither world but exist instead on the margins of both. For others, the gap creates a space in which they can carry out their role using micro-political strategies to achieve their aims. Indeed, Walker found that advisers often widened, rather than reduced, the gap by representing the office as inefficient and bureaucratic when they are in schools and deriding the schools when in the office. This is paradoxical behaviour, for the adviser exists to bridge the gap, and it may be seen as ensuring the advisers' continued existence and at the same time providing them with a larger space within which to operate.

Developing the relationship

Although potentially the relationship with the adviser is very important for the primary head, the structural constraints, inherent contradictions and marginality of the adviser may well act to limit the scope for developing a closer working relationship.

The heads in my case study felt able to turn to their adviser for advice on any topic they liked but the evidence from Winkley's much more substantial study suggests that mine were a fortunate minority. Most of the teachers in his study felt that advisers did not have the skills and experience to be able to assess their schools in depth. Most felt that their adviser knew them and their professional skills only 'a little' or 'hardly at all'. Nearly half of primary teachers had found the most recent visit of an adviser either 'unhelpful' or 'no help at all'. Within these figures there were quite sharp variations which indicate that some advisers are a great deal more successful than others at overcoming the problems inherent in their job. However, Winkley's figures refer to teachers rather than heads and it may be that the heads in Winkley's schools had a rather better opinion of the advisers than did the teachers.

Advisers feel themselves to be working under considerable pressure. Not only are they frequently responsible for a large number of schools (the adviser in my case study was responsible for 95 schools) but the range of tasks is constantly being extended:

> 'There are just too many schools. I used to deal with sixty – that was better and at the time I didn't have as many other things to do.' (Adviser)
>
> (Hill, 1985, p.7)

Appraisal and policing the National Curriculum are yet two more time-consuming tasks which are to be added to the adviser's workload. When advisers on courses talk about their jobs it is clear that they share many of the features of the head's job or indeed of any manager's job. (See Chapter 6) The adviser's job is also characterised by brevity, fragmentation and superficiality, and it too consists of a multiplicity of varied people-centred tasks. It is also clear that the part of their job which brings them most satisfaction is that concerned with change and development (see table on page 38).

It is hardly surprising that advisers facing such difficulties, and having the same need as anyone else for job satisfaction, should use some of their freedom to define their own role in such a way as to develop relationships with some schools rather than with others. Bolam *et al.* (1978) was confirming what many heads suspected when he noted that advisers showed a strong tendency to 'adopt' certain schools and to spend a disproportionate amount of time in those schools.

It has been suggested that all successful social relationships involve an exchange of benefits between those taking part – so-called 'exchange theory' (Blau, 1964). The adopted schools are benefiting in many ways from this close relationship with their adviser, from benefits such as prestige, resources, advice and support. But the advisers too are receiving benefits, which might include job satisfaction, appreciation, a feeling of effectiveness, a reduction in their feeling of not belonging and a reduction in their marginality.

Perhaps it is not too manipulative to suggest that a head who perceives the benefits of a close relationship with the advisory service would do well to consider exchange theory. Above all, heads should see advisers as a resource that are there to be used in the cause of school improvement. They should then seek to make active use of that resource in ways that will benefit the development of the school rather than simply being passive recipients of advisers' advice.

Further reading

Stillman, A. and Grant, M. (1988) *A Study of the LEA Advisory Service*. Windsor: NFER–Nelson. This book gives the results of the only recent large scale research on the role and management of the LEA advisory service.

Winkley, D. (1985) *Diplomats and Detectives – LEA Advisers at Work*. London: Robert Royce. The author is a primary head who studied LEA advisers at work by using interviews, questionnaires and observation. An interesting feature of the book is his discussion of the role of the adviser in relation to the characteristics of the LEA.

CHAPTER 4

Relationships with the DES: the Role of HMI

Even after the full implementation of the Education Act 1988 which gave the Secretary of State some 415 new powers, it is doubtful whether the vast majority of primary schools can be thought to have anything approaching a meaningful relationship with the Department of Education and Science.

The National Curriculum will determine the content of the curriculum, and national testing will check on children's progress through that body of knowledge, but any 'relationship' will be a one-way affair in which the DES hands down the National Curriculum to the schools. Policing of the National Curriculum will be in the hands of the LEA, the governing body and the parents, for, as we shall see, Her Majesty's Inspectorate (HMI) simply do not have the manpower to carry out that task.

Some 10 per cent of primary schools are able to opt out of local authority control by applying for Grant Maintained (GM) status, but even these schools have little by way of direct relationship with the DES. Their grant will be paid by the DES to the school, and the Instrument and Articles of Government will be written by the DES; but in their day to day operation, power will be in the hands of the governing body and head of each school. The curriculum in a GM school must still incorporate the National Curriculum, assessment arrangements will be the same as in the LEA schools, and they will be subject to HMI inspection in the same way as LEA schools. The only part of the management of the school that is likely to involve significantly closer contact with the DES is that of capital spending projects. The school will apply directly to the DES for a 100 per cent grant for eligible projects such as new buildings. The involvement in GM schools of HMI is likely to be only marginally greater than in LEA schools, for the simple reason that no great expansion is envisaged in the number of inspectors.

The role of Her Majesty's Inspectors

What relationship a school has with the DES exists through the contacts with HMI, and in most cases these contacts are very limited. A primary school may expect to be visited by one of Her Majesty's Inspectors once every seven years on average. Most of these visits, however, will be brief and involve only an oral report to the head and to the staff concerned. The visiting HMI will also keep a written record of the visit, which is added to the school's file. This information comes from a reply to a question in the House of Commons given by the then Secretary of State, Sir Keith Joseph. He stated that in 1985 HMI visited approximately 15 per cent of primary schools and 60 per cent of secondary schools in England (Hansard, 24.3.86, p.167). If these visits seem infrequent then full inspections leading to a published report are even less frequent.

During 1986, sixty reports of full inspections of primary schools were published. Because there is normally a delay of several months between inspection and the publication of the report, these schools were not necessarily inspected during 1986, but the figure does give an idea of the number of full inspections of primary schools currently carried out per year. In 1986 the DES statistics show that there were 19,549 primary schools in England. Thus each primary school may expect to be inspected fully once every 325 years or so. In other words most primary heads can safely expect to get through their headship careers of, say, twenty-five years with only a one in 13 chance of being inspected.

Under these circumstances it obviously does not make much sense to speak of a 'relationship' with HMI. They are nonetheless an extremely important and influential elite who tend now to have most influence at the level of the system rather than at the level of the individual school. They occupy a curious position 'in' but not 'of' the Department of Education and Science (DES). They are in a sense independent of both the civil servants and the politicians, being appointed by an Order in Council. However, they are not expected to criticise DES policies in public and, although what they write is published unaltered, the decision of whether to publish rests with the Secretary of State. As the Rayner Report on the Inspectorate notes (DES, 1982), the independence of the Inspectorate, while being highly valued, is also, 'widely misunderstood'. HM Inspectorate has no constitutional independence, for it is the Secretary of State who causes inspections to be carried out. It is, however, the responsibility of the Inspectorate to decide how and what to inspect.

The nature of the HMI's role is also heavily dependent upon the nature of the role of the DES. Thus, during the 1950s and 1960s HMI seemed almost unnecessary because of the non-interventionist role of the DES. Now that each successive Secretary of State is becoming more interventionist than the last, it may well be that the influence of HMI will increase. The establishment of a National Curriculum has finally asserted the right of the DES to hold the key to the door of the 'secret garden' of the curriculum.

The claims of HMIs to expert status are based largely upon their knowledge of the areas of curriculum and pedagogy. Until recently Secretaries of State had eschewed direct control of the curriculum even though the 1944 Act gave them the power to 'control and direct'. Now that the curriculum is seen by both major political parties as a legitimate concern of any Secretary of State, the potential influence of the Inspectorate is greatly increased. As former Senior Chief Inspector Pauline Perry put it:

> No government minister concerned with the quality of education, with the content and pedagogic skill of teachers, could do other than exploit the vast resource of a national Inspectorate with professional expertise and given statutory power to observe the delivery of education every day in classroom, lecture rooms and workshops.
>
> (Perry, 1987)

She goes on to assert that the Inspectorate's independence is vital in order to ensure that they say what they actually observe in schools rather than what others would like them to see. In the recent series of reports by HMI on the effects of government expenditure policies there are signs that the Inspectors are maintaining their independence. Certainly the existence of an independent group of expert professionals, who are prepared to tell the bureaucrats and politicians the truth as they see it, regardless of whether it is palatable, is an invaluable safeguard for heads, teachers and children as we move into this new dirigiste era.

How do HMIs work?

1. Informal visits to schools

Observing what goes on in schools lies at the heart of the Inspector's job. Their advice to the Secretary of State is based upon their observations of what actually happens in schools and colleges. According to the Rayner Report (DES, 1982), visiting such institutions occupies 45 per cent of available HMI time. The figure would be difficult to increase, the report points out, because of the length of the academic year. Most of these visits are informal and lead to nothing more than a 'note of visit' which is held in the file on each school which the Inspectorate keeps.

There are many reasons for such informal visits. It might be that the inspector has a particular interest in an area of the curriculum and wishes to see how the school is tackling 'his' subject. It could be that the inspector is assessing the effectiveness of in-service training. It might be that the school has a high reputation for a particular aspect of its work, say parental involvement or the use of computers. Occasionally it may be that complaints received from parents prompt an informal visit. The note of visit for primary schools contains a number of headings such as: Catchment Area; Accommodation; Equipment and Resources; Organisational Liaison and Continuity; Assessment and Record Keeping; Children With Special Needs; Staff Development and Support; Pastoral Care; and Personal and Social Development of Pupils. The 'work seen' section contains various sub-headings for areas of the curriculum such as Language, Mathematics, Humanities and Science. A further section lists the 'Main Points Made in Discussion with Head'. Unlike the full inspection, these notes are confidential and are not shown to the head or to anyone outside the Inspectorate.

2. *Formal inspections of schools*

Similarly, there are many reasons why a school may be formally inspected. Only a small minority of reporting inspections are prompted by a concern that the school is doing badly. In 1983, the DES suggested that about twenty institutions of all types per year were inspected for this reason:

> The other 250 or so institutions formally inspected each year are either chosen to illustrate particular aspects of education or ways of doing things or are suggested by the computer as part of a sample. In each year the overall provision of two or three local education authorities (LEAs) is considered as the subject of a report.
>
> (DES, 1983)

The first thing a head knows about the selection of the school for a formal inspection is usually a letter giving about two weeks' notice of the inspection. The Reporting Inspector (RI), who leads the team of normally from two to four inspectors, arranges to visit the head. At this visit he explains the purpose of the inspection and discusses the form it will take. He also gives the head a questionnaire about the school to complete prior to the inspection. Currently this questionnaire runs to some twenty-four pages and was reckoned by one RI to take about eighteen hours to complete (Abbott, 1986). The questionnaire covers such topics as:

i a plan of the school and map of its location;
ii the official prospectus, which normally includes a statement of the school's aims and objectives, and a brief account of its history;
iii any statement which the head cared to provide about the school, its particular features and future plans;
iv details of the age, subject and teaching qualifications and experience of each full-time and part-time member of staff and their levels and areas of responsibility;
v the staff handbook, if one exists;
vi a detailed description of the curriculum and organisation of the school (including, in the case of ordinary schools, provision for special eductional needs), its system of communication, the responsibilites of senior and middle management, and the numbers and age groups of pupils;
vii a list of extra-curricular activities (if not covered in the prospectus), with details of those occurring during the inspection;
viii details of capitation funds and their allocation;
ix details of any co-operative teaching arrangement with other institutions;
x a note of any links with contributory and receiving schools, parents, the community and outside agencies (e.g. careers and welfare services, industry);
xi details of any in-service training undertaken by the staff in the last three years;
xii public examination results (where applicable) for at least the last two years, and any analysis or commentaries already to hand;
xiii destinations of leavers over the last two years;
xiv details of ancillary staffing;
xv school, room and class timetables including the times of lessons, and the timetables of individual teachers;
xvi schemes of work for each subject or aspect of the curriculum.

(DES, 1986)

The inspection itself is likely to last from three to five days and involve from two to four Inspectors, depending on the size of the school. The Inspectors will want to see all of the teachers at work with the children. They will also want to look at children's work and talk to them about their work. The inspecting team's interest will also encompass all other aspects of the school's life: assemblies, play-times, dinner-times, extra-curricular activities, and so forth.

Heads and teachers in a small-scale study by Abbott (1986) found the Inspectors inspecting their schools to be courteous and thorough in their investigations, although a majority of the teachers still reported feeling nervous in HMIs' presence. In this study, the Inspectors were seen to be interested in a wide range of topics but Science, Art and Record Keeping were the topics raised most frequently in discussion with the teachers.

At the end of the last full day of inspection the Reporting Inspector discusses with the rest of the team what they have seen and what conclusions they have drawn. The team arrive at a joint view of the school and its performance. A list is drawn up of the points which they wish to put to the head.

On the last day, the team meet with the head and present their findings. The head may choose to have the deputy or any other senior member of staff present at this meeting. Normally this would seem to be a wise course of action since in most schools the deputy will be closely involved in whatever action is considered desirable following the inspection. It will also provide the head with someone with whom he or she can discuss the findings after the Inspectors have left. This meeting is the only opportunity the head will have to correct inaccuracies and to challenge the Inspectors' interpretation of what they have seen. These meetings last for two or three hours and in several of the cases reported by Abbott did lead to modifications in the final published report.

The Reporting Inspector and one other HMI will report their findings to a meeting of the governing body. At this stage the judgements of the Inspectors are not 'open to negotiation' (DES, 1986, p.10). The purpose of the meeting is rather to ensure that the published report 'contains no surprises' (*ibid*).

Several months later – nine on average, according to Sir Keith Joseph (Hansard, 23.3.86 vol. 328) – the head, the clerk to the governors and the Chief Education Officer will each receive a copy of the report. Two weeks later the report is published, with copies being sent to local MPs and the press. Generally, the published reports were seen by Abbott's heads as fair in their praise or criticism of the school, even though a number of minor inaccuracies were contained in the reports. Early press interest in inspection reports seems to have waned, and a primary school report is unlikely to get more than a couple of paragraphs in the local paper. Read in any quantity these reports quickly seem dull. Their careful, measured prose rarely contains anything which is likely to appeal to the readers of the tabloid press.

The published report seems to many heads to contain less criticism and less praise than was provided orally to the head. What is not clear is whether that is a result of the publication of reports since 1983 or whether it was already a feature of the written, as opposed to the oral, report prior to that change of policy. The long delay in publishing most reports certainly seems likely to reduce their impact upon the individual school in terms of its public reputation. In most cases the nine month lapse should have enabled the school to take steps to rectify any shortcomings which had been identified by the inspection process.

Although it is important to remember that the prime purpose of inspection is not to benefit those inspected, HM Inspectors do hope the process of inspection will prove to be a stimulus to the institution to improve the quality of education which it is offering. All of Abbott's heads had positive things to say about being inspected. Generally they welcomed the independent evaluation of their schools by people who had a wide knowledge of schools. Nearly all the heads made specific changes within their schools as a result of the Inspectors' findings. In some cases the inspection seemed to have stimulated action by the LEA, usually in respect of resources. The LEA is in fact routinely asked in a letter accompanying its copy of the report what action it considers is required and what action it proposes to take or has taken in the light of the report. A full inspection report might therefore, under certain circumstances, be an extremely useful document to a headteacher if it adds weight to arguments for additional resources or prompts internal action to improve the effectiveness of the school.

Methods of inspection

HM Inspectorate has often been criticised for the impressionistic nature of the data which they gather. Critics point to the contrast with the way in which educational researchers like the ORACLE team gather data on teaching by using observation schedules, which involve recording the activities of the teacher and certain carefully selected children at specified time intervals. The resulting data are carefully analysed using well-tried statistical techniques before generalisations are made. While such techniques have their place in the researcher's range of methodological approaches, such intensive approaches would not be feasible for HMI to use, given the constraints of time and numbers within which they have to work. Even if such systematic observation were feasible there would remain grave doubts about its appropriateness to the purposes of inspection. The inspection process is intended to provide information of a more holistic nature which depicts, in a more rounded way, the quality of the education that children are receiving in a given school.

It may be that the HMI could learn more profitably from the more ethnographic type of research which attempts to take the participants' views into account. The methods used by the ethnographic researcher and the Inspector are in fact quite similar. Both observe what takes place in the school, both look at work produced by children. Their aims, however, are markedly different. The researcher is seeking to understand the social processes which are taking place in the school. The Inspector is appraising performance. The DES stress in their own booklet on inspections (DES, 1986, p.7) that it is the performance of the children that is being inspected. While the performance of individual teachers is not reported upon, the quality of teaching is assessed. To get inside the life of a school and see the world through the sets of meanings used by those teachers and children is an immensely time-consuming business that would not be a feasible option for the Inspectorate, even if it were appropriate.

So, how do Inspectors inspect? They observe, they listen, they read, they talk and question. They observe what takes place between children and teacher, between child and child, and they observe the conditions under which teaching and learning are taking place. They listen to teachers talking to children, to children talking to one another, and often to children reading. They read schemes of work, records of children's progress, look at displays around the school and, most importantly, they read work produced by children. They talk to children about their work and about school generally, they talk to teachers about their work and about the children. Norman Thomas, the retired Chief Inspector for Primary Schools, who worked his way up through the ranks from primary school teacher, notes wisely that judgements about schools should not be formed too quickly:

> First impressions. . . are on occasion borne out by further observation. But anyone who supposes that they can judge a school within five minutes of entering it should try staying longer more often.
>
> (Thomas, 1983, p.19)

Inspectors do not work to a checklist when inspecting schools. The note of visit contains certain headings, not all of which will necessarily be used for a particular school visit. Visits made in connection with a particular survey may well be structured by the use of an *aide-mémoire* or even a questionnaire, but this is to assist in the collation of information from numerous Inspectors.

However, even a cursory examination of a number of Reports of Inspections of primary schools quickly reveals that some aspects of the schools are discussed in almost every case. Some of these are non-curricular: the atmosphere of the school, the behaviour of the children, the degree of parental involvement. Others relate to aspects of the curriculum: PE, Maths, Topic Work, Language Development, Art and Craft and RE. No doubt the probationary year, when the new Inspector has a 'mentor' and works closely with other Inspectors, is a period of familiarisation with the Inspectorate's *modus operandi* and initiation into how and what to inspect.

How do Inspectors make sense of what they have seen and heard? This is a much more difficult question to answer in detail but, like any other human being, Inspectors bring to bear their own view of reality. This view of the world is the result of the complex interaction of many factors, of which education, gender, ethnic group, upbringing, training, work experiences, values and the social groups to which one belongs, are some of the more important.

Who are the Inspectors?

For most of the first hundred years of its existence the Inspectorate consisted typically of men who had graduated from Oxford or Cambridge. The service exemplified the amateur tradition in British government. The Inspectors were not experts on education. They were 'well-educated', 'fair-minded' members of the Establishment. The Inspectorate now is thoroughly professionalised. The typical advertisement for HMI asks for applicants between 35 and 45 with substantial experience in schools and expertise in a particular aspect of education, usually either a phase or subject specialism. As Sir Keith Joseph put it in reponse to a question in the Commons in 1986:

> The overwhelming majority of Her Majesty's Inspectors are appointed on the basis of proven success as teachers in schools or establishments of further or higher education. . . in exceptional cases, Her Majesty's Inspectors with a non-teaching background may be appointed on the basis of experience in other aspects of education which the inspectorate considers necessary to have within its members.
>
> (Hansard, 24.3.86, 328)

There is, however, one shred of the amateur tradition which survives and which, in view of the way in which the Inspectorate inspect, must cause concern to those involved in primary education. Although in 1986 primary schools constituted 82 per cent of maintained schools and primary pupils constituted slightly over 50 per cent of all maintained school pupils, the indications are that HMIs with experience of primary school teaching were in a very small minority compared with their secondary colleagues. Unfortunately, and somewhat surprisingly, Sir Keith was unable to tell the Commons any details of the inspectors' backgrounds:

> The Department does not maintain in readily accessible form records of all the previous employment of Her Majesty's Inspectors. The detailed information could thus only be provided at disproportionate cost.
>
> (Hansard, 24.3.86, 329)

Thus one is forced to look for clues. The Rayner Report does not address this question directly but it contains a table showing the Regional Deployment of Inspectors and their specialisms. This shows 36 HMI nationally with a specialism in primary schooling out of a total of 407. So in 1981 the primary phase warranted only 11 per cent of the Inspectorate. Perhaps matters have improved since 1981. The only other relevant clue comes from the Secretary of State for Wales who gave the information, in reply to a question in the Commons, that four of the 51 Welsh HMIs had taught in primary schools. A further question elicited the information that this number is even smaller than the number (5) of those who have no experience of teaching in any school at all. Perhaps the Welsh Inspectorate is different but, given the close resemblance in other ways between the two services, there is little reason to believe that they are totally unalike in just this one respect.

Does it matter that so few Inspectors have taught in primary schools? The Secretary of State for Wales thought not. He had:

> . . . no plans to increase the proportion of Her Majesty's Inspectors who have experience of teaching in primary schools.
>
> (Hansard, 24.3.86, p.350)

He claimed that as teacher trainers, LEA advisers or officers they had 'regular contact with primary schools in their former posts', and anyway as HMI they had acquired 'substantial experience of primary schools through inspection visits'. Few primary heads will feel reassured by such claims. It seems to be just another manifestation of the 'Cinderella' status of primary education that inspection of primary schools does not need any direct experience of teaching young children on the part of the Inspectors. It is difficult to imagine a grammar school being happy to be inspected by a team of Inspectors who have worked only in infant schools.

Inspection has loomed large in this discussion of the relationship between the primary head and Her Majesty's Inspectorate but it is important not to lose sight of the Inspectorate's many other, perhaps less immediately visible, activities.

HMI's other activities

Her Majesty's Inspectors are directly involved in mounting in-service courses for teachers, lecturers and advisers. They also organise conferences and contribute to in-service courses arranged by other providers of INSET.

Of increasing importance is their role in producing publications on all aspects of education. These publications draw on their extensive knowledge of what is happening in schools around the country. Some are aimed at people working in the education service, such as the *Curriculum Matters* series. Some are written with a wider readership in mind, such as *Primary Schools, some aspects of good practice* (DES, 1987).

A study of how HMIs used their time was carried out as part of the *Management Review of the Department of Education and Science* (DES, 1979). This found the following distribution of time amongst various activities:

- Visiting educational establishments : 45%
- Office work (of all kinds) : 25%
- Attending meetings and conferences : 20%
- Receiving training, training colleagues or teachers, travelling : 10%

Generally the *Review* found that HMI used their time appropriately, though they expressed some reservations about the amount of time spent in meetings.

Lawton and Gordon, in their illuminating book (Lawton and Gordon, 1987) on Her Majesty's Inspectorate, see the DES as comprising a tri-partite 'mini-tension system' consisting of politicians (ministers, political advisers); bureaucrats (DES officials); and the professionals (HMI). They see each group as characterised by certain beliefs, value and tastes. So the politicians believe in the free market, value freedom of choice and favour independent schools and the payment of fees. The bureaucrats believe in good administration, value efficiency and favour central control, examinations and standard tests. The professionals believe in professionalism, value quality in education and favour impressionistic evaluation. The authors point out that this is, of course, a very simplified view and that some bureaucrats might be closer to the politicians, say, or some HMI may be bureaucratic. After considering the changing role of HMI, Lawton and Gordon conclude:

> It would seem that the move has been made in the direction of greater professionalism rather than closer identification with the DES bureaucracy.
>
> (Lawton and Gordon, 1987, p.126)

Reading what HMI have written about primary education one quickly concludes that the Inspectorate are the professional friends of the primary school:

> The reports indicate that children in these schools are polite and friendly, and that teachers work hard and show care and concern for their pupils. There is much good work in particular subjects but it is too often isolated from work in other curricular areas.
>
> (DES, 1984, p.1)

Friends, in that what they write is supportive and recognises the strengths of primary schools. Professional, in that the criticism is intended to improve practice rather than to pillory. Whether the implementation of the 1988 Act will make HMI more bureaucratic, in Lawton's terms, only time will tell.

Further reading

Lawton, D. and Gordon, P. (1987) *HMI*. London: Routledge and Kegan Paul. Just about the only recent book about the Inspectorate but it provides a fairly full and very readable account of the development and changing role of HMI since its establishment. It also discusses in an analytical way the relationship between the Inspectorate and its political masters.

DES Inspection Reports. (Publications Despatch Centre, DES, Honeypot Lane, Stanmore, Middlesex HA7 1AZ.) The DES runs a publication service which will supply free of charge copies of recent inspection reports on schools. They also have a number of free booklets on HMI methods and procedures. They will take requests by telephone: 01-952 2366.

CHAPTER 5

The Effective Headteacher

The quality of leadership provided by the head is the single most important factor in determining the effectiveness of the school.

The central importance of the headteacher is not only one of the most consistent findings of research but it is also a finding that has been supported repeatedly by committees of enquiry, and one with which parents, teachers, inspectors and children alike would also readily agree. In their study of 'Ten Good Schools' HMI remarked of those schools:

> What they all have in common is effective leadership and a 'climate' that is conducive to growth. . . . Emphasis is laid on consultation, team work and participation, but without exception, the most important single factor in the success of these schools is the quality of leadership.
>
> (DES, 1977, p.36)

To find that everyone regards *you* as the most important determinant of the quality of the whole school can be daunting for a new head; more established heads are merely having their suspicions confirmed. However, centrally important though the head may be this does not mean that he or she is the only important factor. On the contrary, effective heads lead a team which is pulling together towards a clearly articulated goal of excellence. The Thomas Report (ILEA, 1985) describes successful primary heads thus:

> They have not been authoritarian, consultative, or participative as a matter of principle; they have been all three at different times as the conditions seem to warrant, though most often participative. Their success has often come from choosing well, from knowing when to take the lead and when to confirm the leadership offered by their colleagues.
>
> (ILEA, 1985, p.66)

The picture then of the successful head is quite different from that of the traditional authoritarian leader, the one who might have used King's memorably adapted phrase: 'L'école, c'est moi'.

It would have been possible to devote this entire book to the topic of leadership – indeed in a sense that has been done, for it runs like a thread throughout every chapter. However, here I wish to make it more explicit and consider briefly what is meant by leadership, the various styles a head may adopt, the relative strengths and weaknesses of these styles, and to consider in more detail just what it is that effective heads actually do.

What is leadership?

This looks like a simple enough question. As we have seen, everyone seems to recognise effective leadership when they see it, or the lack of it when they are unlucky enough to have endured it. However, defining leadership is no easy matter and has exercised many minds:

> (There)... are almost as many different definitions of leadership as there are persons who have attempted to define the concept.
>
> (Stogdill, 1974, p.7)

My personal preference would be for Katz and Kahn's definition:

> We consider the essence of organisational leadership to be the influential increment over mechanical compliance with the routine directions of the organisation.
>
> (Katz and Kahn, 1966, p.302)

The headteacher of a British primary school does after all possess more legal authority to direct the labour of others, both staff and children, than almost any other holder of a public office. However, no head is likely to be successful in running an effective school if he or she relies primarily upon that legal authority. The use of a legal authority is likely to secure no more than the mechanical compliance referred to above. What every head is aiming to do is to secure that 'influential increment', to harness people's energies and enthusiasms to the purposes of the school, to get staff to 'go the extra mile'. The frequent reliance upon the legal authority of the head is often seen by all as evidence of a failure of leadership. While it may be appropriate on certain occasions to rely upon that authority, most heads will seek other ways to exercise leadership even though their legal authority will always be there in the background.

Studies of leadership

Early studies of leadership tended to focus on the personality characteristics of the leader in isolation from either the led or the situation in which the leading was to be done. Such an approach generated tests of personal qualities which effective leaders displayed: for example, self-confidence, high energy level, determination and flexibility.

It soon became apparent that the nature of people to be led must also be considered. The human relations school studied the characteristics of the work group and found that such qualities as their 'viscidity' (how much the group cohered) and 'hedonic tone' (how much they tried to enjoy themselves) were important (Hemphill, 1949).

From this approach there developed an interest in the behaviour of the leader and the led. One of the chief proponents of this approach (Halpin, 1966) devised a questionnaire to classify leaders according to the degree to which they emphasised patterns of organisational procedures (initiating structure) and warmth in the relationships between leader and led (consideration).

The current approach is to stress that there is no single, most effective leadership style. This contingency approach sees choice of leadership style as contingent upon the characteristics of the leader, the led, and the task to be undertaken. Thus Landers and Myers concluded in a paper included in a widely-used Open University course reader:

> There is enough research evidence now, however, to confirm that there is no one style that is universally effective in every situation. . . no one style is always better than another. Various styles are effective in various situations; there is no ideal style.
>
> (Landers and Myers, 1977, p.149)

If years of theorising and research have come to that conclusion then, one might ask, what does that mean for practising headteachers facing the often conflicting and always pressing demands of running a school? The message for once seems clear: effective headteachers would do well to have available a repertoire of leadership styles which may be deployed according to the situation in which they find themselves. The views expressed in the earlier quote from the Thomas Report are a clear example of the contingency approach to leadership. It is an approach which Handy (1985) has described as the 'best fit'. Four factors need to be considered: the leader, the subordinates, the task and the environment.

Styles of leadership

Leaders tend to have preferred leadership styles which derive in the main from their personality characteristics. Many writers have

Leadership Categories

LEWIN (1944)	*AUTOCRATIC*	*DEMOCRATIC*	*LAISSEZ-FAIRE*
NIAS, J. (1980) 'Leadership Styles and Job Satisfaction in Primary Schools'. In BUSH, T. *et al*. Eds. (1980) *Approaches to School Management*. London: Harper & Row/OUP	**Bourbon** Inefficient administration. Treats individual teachers as inferiors. Does not encourage or allow participation in goal-setting and decision-making.	**Positive** Sets high professional standards. High level of personal involvement. Readily available especially for discussion. Interested in individual teacher development. Gives lead in establishing school aims. Encourages participation in goal-setting and decision-making.	**Passive** Sets low professional standard. Low level of personal involvement. Does not monitor teachers' standards. Inefficient administration. Not easy to contact or talk to. Does not support individual teachers. Has no perceived aims.
WATERS, D. (1979) *Management and Headship in the Primary School*. London: Ward Lock.	**I Autocratic** Authoritarian, formal, inflexible, rule-bound, punitive, coercive, hierarchical and bureaucratic. **II Paternal** Benevolent despot: kindly interest and regard for staff who do not dissent. Receives love and loyalty.	**Democratic** Informed and relaxed, encourages personal initiative, delegates real responsibility, encourages group approach to problem-solving, creates good working atmosphere.	**Laissez-faire** Abdicates authority and responsibility. Everyone does their own thing. Little or no guidance from head. May hide behind administrative work.

LEWIN (1944)	*AUTOCRATIC*	*DEMOCRATIC*	*LAISSEZ-FAIRE*
COULSON, A. A. (1976) 'The Role of the Primary Head'. In PETERS, R. S. Ed. (1976) *The Role of the Head*. London: Routledge & Kegan Paul.	**Paternalistic** Ego identification with the school – leading by personal precept and example. Head filters outside influences on school. Pervasive control of curriculum and pedagogy. Limited delegation – head responsible for all aspects of the school.	**Collegial** Head as chief executive. Leadership based on rational influence rather than institutionalised supremacy.	
BALL, S. J. (1987) *The Micro-Politics of the School*. London: Methuen.	**Political: I Adversarial** Stress on open debate and discussion but head's view prevails. **Political: II Authoritarian** Head asserts – opposition is avoided, disabled or ignored. Common in long serving heads maintaining status quo. **Interpersonal**: informal relationships, lines of obligation and exchange maintained through the person of the head.	**Managerial** A form of bureaucratic control. Head relates to staff through a management team and a formal structure of meetings and committees. Written documentation specifies roles and responsibilities. Head runs school from the office but still dominates. Junior staff feel excluded from decision making.	

LEWIN (1944)	*AUTOCRATIC*	*DEMOCRATIC*	*LAISSEZ-FAIRE*
LLOYD, K. (1985) 'Management and Leadership in the Primary School'. In HUGHES, M. *et al*. (1985) *Managing Education*. London: Holt, Rinehart and Winston.	**Paternal** Active and dominant influence in school. Led by example. Consultation rather than participation but head's view prevails. (30%) **Coercive** Imposes views without consultation or participation – strong task orientation. (8%) Total: 38%	**Extended Professional** Collaborative approach, stress on professional development, participation in decision making, friendly and informal relationships. Total: 42%	**Nominal** Lack of trust and respect, disengaged head. (2%) **Passive** Remote and isolated, with any initiatives coming from staff. (4%) **Familiar** High on consideration low on structure – stressed autonomy of class teacher. (14%) Total: 20%
HANDY, C. and AITKEN, R. (1986) *Understanding Schools as Organisations*. Harmondsworth: Penguin.	**Club Culture** Organisation is there to extend the person of the head who would do everything himself if he could. Informal structure. **Role Culture** School as a set of roles – formal organisation and structure.	**Task Culture** Cooperative groups of colleagues working on problem with little hierarchical organisation.	**Personal Culture** Stress on individual autonomy with minimal organisation.

produced descriptions of the various leadership styles used by head-teachers. While there are minor differences, the majority are not far removed from Lewin's (1944) classification of autocratic; democratic; and laissez-faire. Two more recent studies (Nias, 1980; Lloyd, 1985) carried out specifically on English primary heads, fit fairly easily into Lewin's categories, while using more colourful titles for the styles. The key difference in each case seems to be the degree to which heads take decisions on their own without consulting their staff – that is, the degree of participation in decision making which they encourage.

Many writers have produced typologies of leadership styles for varying purposes, a number of which are very briefly summarised in the table. Although these have been organised under the headings devised by Lewin, it is important to note that the degree of fit is not always especially close. It should be noted, too, that Handy and Aitken (1986) are describing the cultures which result to some degree from the head's leadership style rather than describing the style directly. It can be amusing as well as instructive to see how one's own leadership behaviour and that of heads one has known fit the various categories. It would not be surprising to find that any particular individual fitted more than one category. Indeed, contingency theory would suggest that an effective head would use a repertoire of styles, adjusting the style to the task, the followership and the situation. The test of an effective use of the contingent approach would be how appropriate the style was in a particular set of circumstances.

Participation in decision making

One of the principal difficulties for heads in adopting a contingent approach is that of identifying the particular level of participation which a specific decision needs. Mortimore *et al.* (1988) addressed this problem when considering how heads should respond to their findings on junior school effectiveness, though they seem to offer little comfort:

> They need to be able to divide the decisions which they are required to make into two groups: those which it is quite properly their responsibility to take and for which any attempt at delegation to a staff decision would be seen as a dereliction of duty, and those which, equally properly, belong to the staff as a whole. In some cases it will be perfectly clear to which group a certain decision belongs; in others, it will be extremely difficult to decide. Mistakes will be made and the consequences. . . will have to be suffered.
>
> (Mortimore *et al.*, 1988, p.281)

A second problem arises from the fact that teachers vary in terms of the amount of participation in decision making that they want. Some early work carried out in the United States (Belasco and Alutto, 1972) suggests that some teachers will feel 'decisionally deprived' while others will be suffering from 'decisional saturation'. They found this to be related to such factors as age and gender, with younger men more likely to be getting less participation than they want while older women are more likely to be expected to participate to a greater degree than they want. However, that picture is too simple to provide a reliable guide to action.

A school that has had a laissez-faire or autocratic head is likely to have a staff of teachers who have been denied the opportunity to participate in decision making. A group approach to problem solving is likely to take time to become established where there is no tradition of working in that way. It may take time to convince the whole staff that it is worth investing the extra time and energy that a more collaborative approach demands. No one is likely to be convinced if the task they are working on is regarded as one which the head is paid to deal with, or one which is seen as unimportant. Nor is participation going to be seen as worthwhile if the teachers believe that the participation is just a sham. The last point raises another real dilemma since, statutorily, responsibility for managing the school rests with the head: in the final analysis it is the head who is answerable for what happens within the school. How can these problems be resolved?

Some areas of the school's activities are regarded by teachers as of particular importance to them. They are the ones that are seen as central to their role as teachers – such matters as the selection of textbooks, the construction and implementation of curriculum guidelines, ways of organising teaching and learning in the classroom. These, then, would be suitable areas of decision making for the head to employ a more democratic leadership style. If the teaching staff are new to that style of leadership then the head would do well not to embark upon all of these areas at once. It might be a good strategy to select an area of the curriculum where the teachers feel they have less expertise – say science – for here the risks of encountering entrenched positions are less than with an area such as reading where every primary teacher feels they are, or should be, an authority.

The problem of ensuring that the teachers feel they are genuinely participating while the head retains ultimate responsibility is more difficult. The key may be found in Nias's (1980) work, which looked at the connection between job satisfaction and the head's leadership style. The teachers in her study expected the head to set the overall values of the school but wanted to participate in goal setting and decision making. The message seems to be that the head should give a professional lead and determine those overall values (that is, establish a 'mission' and set the climate of the school) while encouraging teachers to participate in the decisions necessary for translating those values into practice within the school. Openness rather than deviousness is the best strategy for the head who wants to encourage participation. The head should make clear the limits within which the participation is to take place and then adopt a genuinely democratic position within these limits.

Why encourage participation?

If a democratic leadership style is fraught with such problems why bother to adopt it? Coulson (1976) – with considerable insight probably born of hard experience – has pointed out that a paternalistic headship style diminishes the professionality of primary school teachers. He points out that the teachers will not develop as professionals who assume full responsibility for their work unless a head uses a more democratic or 'collegial' leadership style which relies on rational influence. Thus one of the most powerful arguments for participation rests upon the desirability of developing the teachers' professionality from what Hoyle (1974) described as 'restricted professionality' towards 'extended professionality'. (See Chapter 13 for a fuller discussion of professional development.)

There are other arguments which have to do more directly with improving the school's effectiveness. Management theory has long been concerned with the role of the professional in an organisation, and how to get the right compromise between autonomy and the demands of the organisation. The conclusion of most of this work has been that professionally staffed organisations like schools need to allow scope for autonomy for teachers if they are to perform effectively. Professionals give of their best in an organisation which allows them some say in determining their own work.

Again this poses a dilemma for a head, who will also be concerned that there is continuity and progression in the children's work as they move from class to class through the school. For once this is a relatively easily resolved dilemma. There is a paradox inherent in a democratic leadership style: participation in decision making simultaneously increases teachers' control while reducing their autonomy. If teachers have been fully involved in framing a new policy document on science it is then much more likely that the new policy will actually determine to some degree their practice in the classroom. Having agreed with one's colleagues upon certain policies, it is then far harder to go away to the classroom and quietly ignore them than it is to ignore some guideline imposed, without participation, by the head. While a policy agreed in this way may not be exactly what the head would have produced alone, it does at least stand a much better chance of being implemented, rather than joining the dusty collection of ignored documents to be found in any teacher's cupboard.

Delegation

All children, most parents, and many teachers still expect the headteacher to know everything about everything. The head is expected to be an expert on everything from teaching reading to infants to extending mathematics skills in high fliers, taking in music, PE, RE, art and project work on the way. In addition to curricular expertise, there are innumerable other areas where the head is expected to have the answer. While this may initially be somewhat flattering, few sane heads will honestly believe themselves to be omniscient. There will be members of staff who have greater knowledge of, and expertise in, certain areas of the curriculum. Even where heads do feel competent to make decisions on their own in all areas of the school's activities, they are quickly going to experience a severe sense of overload if they insist on taking sole responsibility for every aspect of the school's organisation. The impossibility of possessing sufficient knowledge, expertise, wisdom and sheer energy to meet fully the multitude of often conflicting demands of headship is another powerful reason for adopting a more collegial style of leadership and delegating responsibilities to other members of staff who have the knowledge, expertise and motivation to take them on.

The delegating of responsibilities to other teachers should also be seen as a valuable way of promoting their professional development. The deputy head is in a particularly strong position both to take on such delegated responsibilities and to benefit professionally from them. The majority of deputies are heads in training, and should be given opportunities to take responsibility which will further their development.

Managing participation

It would be misleading, however, to suggest that there are no disadvantages to a democratic leadership style. Perhaps the most significant one is that it can be immensely time-consuming. Teachers' time is probably the most precious resource that the school has available with which to accomplish its aims. It is vital therefore that teacher time is not squandered in endless discussions and staff meetings which do not result in action based on a sound consensus. The efficient management of teacher time spent on participative decision making must be a priority for heads who adopt a democratic leadership style. Formerly it was perfectly possible for teachers to refuse to attend staff meetings if they so wished; with directed hours, that possibility fortunately no longer exists. However, it would be disastrous for effective democratic leadership if a head used the new powers to direct teachers to attend meetings that are not seen to be valuable.

Managing staff meetings

While the small scale of most primary schools makes bureaucratic procedures inappropriate, some of the more formal aspects of running meetings should be considered, to see if they could help make the staff meeting more effective.

Should staff meetings have agendas? Many primary heads feel uncomfortable with such formal arrangements but an agenda can be useful even in a relatively small school. Provided the agenda is issued in advance it does at least let everyone know the purpose of the meeting, and gives them an opportunity to reflect in advance on the topics which are to be discussed. So long as the agenda is actually used in the meeting itself, it also ensures that the meeting stays 'on task' instead of meandering ineffectually over a range of irrelevant matters. There should be an opportunity for any of the teachers to suggest additional agenda items. Heads should resist any temptation to be devious over the building of the agenda because sooner or later they are going to be found out and will endanger the whole process of fostering a participative climate by making participation appear a sham.

The keeping of minutes is another procedure which tends to be associated with formality and may thus be rejected by many primary heads. However, it is worth considering the advantages of keeping minutes before rejecting them as running counter to the informal atmosphere of the primary school. Minutes kept in an open and honest way, copies of which are then circulated without delay to all the staff, provide a durable record of what the meeting decided. This helps to reduce ambiguity and the effects of selective memory loss. Minutes also enable staff who missed meetings to catch up on what happened. A useful technique for keeping minutes during a meeting is to use a flip chart and thick felt tip pen. A recorder, other than the chairman, records significant points and decisions on the flip chart for all to see. This enables the record to be challenged if people feel their point has been misrepresented or ignored. It can also help to keep the discussion clearly focused. The flip chart sheets then become the basis upon which the minutes are written after the meeting.

A frequent criticism of staff meetings made by teachers is that they tend to go on too long. This results in feelings of resentment against the waste of time and against the open-ended nature of the commitment. It can also result in people trying to win by attrition rather than by rational argument. A realistic guillotine is a useful procedure to resolve these difficulties. A simple rule that no staff meeting may last longer than, say, one and a half hours can be effective.

Reviewing the Conduct of the Staff Meeting

- Was everyone clear about the purpose of the meeting?
- Did I manage to draw everyone into the discussion?
- Did I accept and value everyone's contribution?
- Did I listen?
- Did I correctly summarise the group's views?
- Did the group stay on task without being so tightly controlled that contributions were stifled?
- Did the recorded decisions truly reflect the views of the group?
- How well did I handle conflicting views?
- Was my body language positive?
- Was the tone of the meeting relaxed without being frivolous?
- Was everyone clear about what was decided?
- Was everyone clear about what action they were to take as a consequence of the decisions?

Even more important than the ground rules is the way in which the head conducts the meeting itself. Running meetings is an area of management where heads can, and do, learn to improve their performance. Deputies too should have an opportunity to learn these skills by being given responsibility for running some of the staff meetings. After the meeting it would be valuable for the head and deputy to discuss each other's performance in the chair. Some of the questions worth considering have been listed.

The head as cultural leader

A recent study of the staff relationships in five primary schools carried out by a group from the Cambridge Institute of Education (Nias *et al.*, forthcoming) found that each school had its own culture in the sense of shared beliefs and ways of doing things. Although many people exercised leadership, including the school secretary, the chief leader was the headteacher.

The school was seen as 'belonging' to the headteacher, and heads often spoke of 'my school'. They were expected by the staff to embody the values of the school and to exemplify those values in their personal and professional behaviour. The heads in this study created a 'culture of collaboration' by:

> . . . the use of assembly to make explicit the underlying beliefs, values, and aims of the head (and his/her deputy); the personal example of the head and deputy. . . the use of a shared language. . . extensive use of humour; the creation of a comfortable staffroom. . . very careful staff selection; purposeful initiation of newcomers.
>
> (Nias *et al.*, forthcoming)

Job satisfaction

Keeping the teachers happy is not enough on its own to produce a staff with high morale, let alone a school which is performing at maximum effectiveness. Some features of the laissez-faire styles of leadership derive from an anxiety on the part of the head not to upset anyone, but teachers require something more than that if they are to experience job satisfaction, as Nias (1980) found. Teachers' job satisfaction comes mainly from effective teaching, from a feeling that they are getting the job done, that children are making progress in their learning. In a school where the head is disengaged, where children's learning and teachers' standards are not monitored, where eveyone does their own thing with little or no guidance from the head – where, in short, the head abdicates his or her authority and responsibility – children make less progress in their learning and the staff derive no job satisfaction.

Effective leadership and effective schools

There is a burgeoning field of research in North America into school effectiveness. To date there is only one substantial home-grown primary example, the *Junior School Project* (Mortimore *et al.*, 1988) which followed 2,000 junior pupils through four years in 50 different London primary schools. The findings from this study are unequivocal about the connection between effective leadership by the head and the level of effectiveness of the school. 'Purposeful leadership of the staff by the headteacher' appears as one of the twelve key factors associated with more effective schools.

What exactly did purposeful heads do? According to Mortimore *et al.* (1988), purposeful heads:

- are actively involved in the school's work
- do not exert total control over their staff
- understand the needs of the school
- are involved with staff in curriculum discussions
- influence the content of curriculum guidelines without taking complete control
- selectively influence teaching strategies
- receive forecasts of teachers' work plans
- monitor pupils' progress through teachers keeping individual records
- emphasise praise and reward rather than punishment
- encourage INSET attendance for good reason
- involve the deputy head in decision making and planning
- involve teachers in decision making and planning

It is interesting that these findings are very much in line with the findings of much more extensive research from North America on the relationship between the head's behaviour and school effectiveness. The role of the elementary school principal in the USA is rather different from that of the English primary school head, in that he or she tends to be rather more of an administrator who is less actively involved as a leading professional. However the research findings all suggest that a move towards the English model would make the schools more effective.

Persell and Cookson (1982) reviewed more than seventy-five studies of effective principals and found a high level of agreement on nine features of the behaviour of good principals.

The Effective Principal in Action

(1) Demonstrating a commitment to academic goals
(2) Creating a climate of high expectations
(3) Functioning as an instructional leader
(4) Being a forceful and dynamic leader
(5) Consulting effectively with others
(6) Creating order and discipline
(7) Marshalling resources
(8) Using time well
(9) Evaluating results

Source: Persell and Cookson (1982)

On this subject there is a remarkably high degree of consistency between the findings of research and the current conventional wisdom about what good heads do. All of which makes it even more surprising that, according to Lloyd (1985), less than half (42 per cent) of the primary heads in his sample were actually leading their schools using what he called an 'extended professional' style of leadership.

In Canada, Leithwood and Montgomery (1986) have produced a 'profile' of the effective principal. It is particularly interesting because it is arranged in four levels of effectiveness and the authors argue that heads should be helped to develop towards the fourth, most effective, level.

Four Levels of Principal Effectiveness

Level One: The Administrator He sees the principal's job as organising the routine activities of the school while teachers see to the teaching. In decision making he is reactive, autocratic, inconsistent and aims to maintain order. He derives his expectations and knowledge primarily from his own personal experience.

Level Two: The Humanitarian He sees the principal's job as making sure all the teachers are happy and stresses the importance of interpersonal relationships. He encourages participation in decision making because that increases staff contentment and he is proactive on interpersonal relationships, reactive on other matters. He derives his expectations and knowledge mostly from his own personal experiences and beliefs.

Level Three: The Program Manager He sees the principal's job as implementing effective programmes in the classroom and uses a limited number of tried and tested strategies to this end. They use several forms of decision making depending upon the urgency of the decision but seek to involve staff. He derives his expectations and knowledge largely from his own experience but also from public sources including the occasional research report.

Level Four: The Systematic Problem Solver He sees the principal's job as pursuing highly ambitious goals for all pupils. These goals are transformed into short term plans and they work for consistency among the staff. In decision making he is skilled in many forms and matches the form to the setting, while working towards high levels of participation by teachers. He anticipates a high proportion of the decisions to be made. He derives his expectations and knowledge from research, his own professional judgement and that of other respected professionals.

Adapted from: Leithwood and Montgomery (1986)

Only some 10 per cent of the Canadian principals which Leithwood and Montgomery studied operated for most of the time at level four. The challenge for headteachers, and those involved in helping headteachers to improve their performance, is to find ways of moving performance on to the next level. The first step is to identify at which level one normally operates; here a trusted fellow head or respected adviser could be very helpful since self-diagnosis can be difficult in practice. The next step is to select an aspect of one's performance as a head and devise a strategy for moving that aspect on to the next level. The idea that leaders are born needs laying to rest: leadership may be developed.

Hodgkinson (1983) sees the leader as having four responsibilities: know the task; know the situation; know your followership; know yourself. I would suggest a fifth responsibility: develop yourself.

Further reading

Leithwood, K. A. and Montgomery, D. J. (1986) *Improving Principal Effectiveness: The Principal Profile*. Toronto: Ontario Institute for Studies in Education Press. Although Canadian in origin there is a great deal here which is of direct relevance to English heads who wish to develop their own management practice. The authors have drawn extensively on their own and other people's research to construct their four levels of effectiveness.

Mortimore, P. *et al.*, (1988) *School Matters, the Junior Years*. Wells: Open Books. This book reports the findings of the Junior School Project on factors affecting the progress of 2,000 pupils over the four years of junior schooling. It contains a wealth of information about the features of effective schools that all heads should know about.

CHAPTER 6

Managing One's Own Time

Heads on management courses often carry out some sort of 'diary exercise' in which they keep a close record of how they spend their own time in school and then analyse the results in terms of the number, duration and purpose of their activities. Most are distressed at their findings. Typically, they find that they spend most of their time on very brief, often interrupted, apparently minor tasks. Now this is rarely a revelation of something they were unaware of. Most heads realise that they often get bogged down in activities which they feel they ought not to be doing, but frequently there is no one else to do them. Most also realise that many of their activities are interrupted, sometimes briefly, sometimes so substantially that they are unable to return to complete the original task. So it is not so much the revelatory nature of the diary exercise which is distressing but the fact that it confirms one's worst suspicions about where the days have gone.

Managers at work in commerce and industry

Many studies have been carried out on how managers in commerce and industry use their time. There are several substantial studies of how secondary heads fill their days, but the studies of primary heads are both few in number and small in scale. The interesting thing about these various studies, however, is that they show a remarkable degree of consistency in their findings about how these different managers go about their jobs. Of course, the substantive content of their managerial roles differs greatly but the characteristic features of *how* the job is done are strikingly similar.

Rosemary Stewart (1967) studied 160 British senior and middle managers for a period of four weeks using a self-report diary method.

She found that the managers' day was made up of many varied activities, few of which lasted very long and many of which were interrupted by other people; but only a very small part of that time was spent with their superiors.

In the United States, Henry Mintzberg (1973) observed the work of five male Chief Executives and found that their work too was '. . . characterized by brevity, variety and fragmentation' (p.31). His influential book *The Nature of Managerial Work* reports the findings of this study but also draws upon a wealth of other data gathered by many researchers who have studied managers at work. Although virtually all of these studies focus upon managers in commercial and industrial organisations, it is remarkable how many primary heads would find that Mintzberg's views of the manager's life correspond directly to their own experience of life as a headteacher.

Mintzberg saw managerial work as comprising three areas and ten associated roles. The first area was to do with people, the **interpersonal**. The roles associated with this area were those of figurehead, leader and liaison. The second area was to do with information, the **informational**. In this connection the roles were of monitor, disseminator and spokesman. The final area was to do with making decisions, the **decisional**. Here the roles were entrepreneur, disturbance handler, resource allocator and negotiator. Most heads would easily be able to see their job in those terms. The only problem is that so could a great number of other people who are not what we would normally consider to be managers. For example, the primary head who has a young family might be able to see his or her weekend life at home as comprising those areas and those roles too. If this is the case then it would seem that the framework does not capture the distinctive features of managerial work *per se*. In other words, this categorisation is not distinguishing very accurately between managerial work activities and the other activities of life.

Heads might also recognise in their own jobs most of the distinguishing characteristics of managerial work which Mintzberg noted:

- Much work at unrelenting pace
- Activity characterised by brevity, variety and fragmentation
- Preference for live action
- Attraction to the verbal (oral) media
- Link between their organisation and a network of contacts
- Blend of rights and duties (puppet and puppeteer)

Many other studies of managers in commercial and public service organisations have reached similar conclusions about what it is that managers do at work, and the similarities with the work of the head-teacher are striking.

What do secondary heads do all day?

Lyons (1974) carried out a very substantial study of heads and senior staff in secondary schools. His principal method was the self-report diary. These were completed by 513 staff in 16 schools spread over one year. He collected 8,000 diary returns containing over 100,000 diary entries; these generated over 2,000,000 items of information which he coded into some 600 categories. Lyons' analysis of the activities on which secondary heads spend their time shows clear similarities with other studies of the activities of primary heads although there are, of course, some differences. Thus both types of head found themselves spending time on 'routine administration and office duties' or 'teaching, marking and lesson preparation' whereas 'pupil careers and tertiary education' and 'internal and external examinations' feature highly only for secondary heads. However, it is not so much the content of the activities that is relevant to this discussion as the form or characteristic features of those activities. It's not so much what they do as the way they do it, to paraphrase the song.

Lyons found that the head's day was people-intensive, that it covered a wide variety of activities of brief duration and was subject to constant interruption, with even the interruptions being interrupted. The more senior the teacher, the greater the number of unanticipated events occurring in his or her day, with the head having the most interruptions and the largest proportion of activities of short duration. These features had serious implications for the effective execution of the head's role:

> ... priorities break down in the face of continual pressure of events until the work assumes the pattern of crisis administration.... Priorities are re-assigned on the basis of the duration of events and the longer events migrate towards the end of the day....
>
> (Lyons, 1974, p.300)

Nor can we reassure ourselves with the thought that this research was carried out some time ago and the relatively recent innovation of management training courses for heads has led to an improvement. Hall *et al.*'s (1986) study which observed fifteen secondary heads for a day and a further four for a school year concluded:

> ... we found that little had changed in the scope and character of heads' performance of the job since Lyons' (1974) description of its fragmentary quality.
>
> (Hall *et al.*, 1986, p.206)

The picture which they paint of the head's day is indeed familiar:

> The main features in the working day are: fragmentation of activity, i.e. heads carry out a large number of different acts; people intensive, i.e. heads interact with a variety of people; and range of tasks, i.e. educational, administrative and managerial activities both internal and external to the school.
>
> (Hall *et al.*, 1986, p.11)

They also found that heads tended to spend very little time on educational policy and curricular matters where they did not actually schedule meetings to discuss such activities. This is a particularly interesting point if one is considering how to manage time more effectively. It seems clear that unless time is specifically set aside for those important management activities, they will be pushed aside by other, more immediately pressing, matters.

What do primary heads do all day?

What primary heads actually do has not been the object of substantial research, although analysis seems to be a popular activity for management training courses seeking to improve the effectiveness with which heads use their time. There are a few small-scale studies of primary heads which rely typically on self-report diaries kept by the heads. Unfortunately, they all use different ways of categorising the activities so it is rather difficult to draw firm conclusions about how heads do in fact use their time.

In Clerkin's (1985) sample, new heads were most frequently involved in face to face communication with teachers and pupils and in carrying out general administration. Overall he found their days to be characterised by 'a high intensity of tasks with frequent interruptions'. He noted that this created a situation where most of the head's attention went to 'keeping the school ticking over' with relatively little attention being given to longer term issues. In his view:

> They seem to have become over-involved at times with relatively minor tasks rather than delegating these to other appropriate persons.
>
> (Clerkin, 1985)

This is an interesting point for those concerned about how heads might improve their use of time. It is a point found repeatedly in the research evidence: primary heads are reluctant to delegate even minor tasks to their staff.

In Davies's (1987) study, which used a very small sample of heads, we find a familiar pattern. They also had days which were typically '...characterised by brevity, variety and fragmentation'. They averaged 50 tasks per day, each task lasting an average 13 minutes. Nearly half of their time was spent in classrooms and 20 per cent of their time on administrative tasks. He also observed that the heads seemed to be at the centre of an information network, with most decisions, even minor ones, being referred to them. While this put them in an excellent position to know what was going on throughout the school, it seems to indicate that these heads at least were no different from the paternal heads which Coulson (1976) regarded as having a diminishing effect on their teachers' professionality.

The message from these two studies, and it is repeated elsewhere, is that heads fail to distinguish between minor tasks which could and should be delegated, and major tasks which only the head can perform. Hall *et al.* (1986) noticed the same phenomenon with their sample of secondary heads, who tended to respond to all problems as though they were equally important and so got involved in a mass of minor matters. Heads of small schools may have difficulty in finding people to whom they can delegate tasks, but most heads do not have that problem. Delegation does not just help the head to make more appropriate use of his time but it also offers the staff opportunities to take responsibility in a way that enhances their professionality.

An interesting feature of Harvey's (1986) study was that he asked his sample of primary heads to record how they had *planned* to spend their time as well as how they had actually spent it. This enabled him to examine the extent to which what they did diverged from what they had intended to do. It will come as no surprise to a practising head to find that part of the unplanned workload resulted from unanticipated teacher absences which required the head to act at short notice as a supply teacher. However, the unplanned element resulted much more from unanticipated visits from LEA advisers and parents, and from visits which extended longer than expected. Heads of small schools (here defined as four teachers or less) spent a much greater proportion of their time in contact with pupils because they had at least a part-time teaching responsibility for a class. These heads also spent less time with other teaching staff, due partly no doubt to the smaller numbers of such staff but also to the reduced opportunities for contact caused by the heads' teaching commitments. This class teaching responsibility is one of the major constraints upon heads of small schools in carrying out their managerial role. In fact, most small school heads experience considerable role conflict between their roles of class teacher and head-teacher.

A study of an Australian primary head and his deputy by Gronn (1983) takes as its starting point the finding by so many other studies that heads spend their time at work in contact with other people. Gronn analysed closely the conversations between the head and his deputy as they made decisions about which teacher should teach which class in the next school year. He found that 'talk is the work' of the headteacher.

> The analysis shows that not only do administrators spend much of their time talking and that this talk accomplishes administration, but that talk is used to do the work of tightening and loosening administrative control.
>
> (Gronn, 1983, p.289)

So heads' work necessarily involves contact with people: it is through people, of course, that the head gets the work done.

When Acker (1988) observed a primary head intermittently for a period of more than a year she too found that the head's days were hectic, full of unanticipated events and were spent with people. However, in her view, these features of the job, far from being de-moralising, were actually sources of job satisfaction for the head:

> The interruptions and unexpected events were themselves exciting and lent variety and challenge to the work. . . . The people-oriented side of the job was a key source of pleasure. Children were central. When I asked in interview what the satisfactions were in her job, she immed-iately spoke about the children. . . .
>
> (Acker, 1988, p.34)

What emerges from these studies is a somewhat daunting picture of the primary head's fragmented day with the brief, people-centred activities of an immediate short-term nature getting interrupted by unanticipated events and visitors. In this, primary heads are no different from their colleagues in the secondary school. Furthermore both primary and secondary heads differ little, in this respect at least, from managers in commerce and industry.

So, does it matter? Given the head's pivotal position in the school the answer must clearly be yes. One could adapt Mintzberg's (1973) observation and say that to be superficial is an occupational hazard for headteachers. If their attention is constantly absorbed by brief, pressing problems of immediate concern, then when are they carrying out the higher level management activities which everyone assumes them to be doing? As Lyons remarked:

> Occupying as he does a central position within the school's organisation, he is the one person to have a holistic impression and becomes the coordinator of activities, the planner, responsible for the shape of the organisation; or at least he would if the pressure of events did not overwhelm him.
>
> (Lyons, 1974, p.36)

Given what we know about the importance of the way that heads do their jobs in terms of school effectiveness, it is clearly important that they should manage their own time in such a way that the pressure of events does not overwhelm them. Management for effectiveness should be the goal, not mere crisis management. So, how can heads go about improving their own time management?

Five questions to ask oneself

1. What am I currently doing with my time?

The first step is to record and analyse how one is currently using one's time and probably the easiest way of doing this is to use a diary or log. One of the problems of keeping a diary is that it tends to record single acts when those single acts actually have multiple significance. For example, a head praises a child's piece of work. That would probably be regarded as a brief interaction with a pupil, and it may also be recorded as an interruption if at that time the head was already speaking to the caretaker about the state of the children's toilets. Yet this interaction is also an example of what Americans call 'instructional management' (Bossert, 1986) in which the head may be helping to set standards of academic excellence and shape the school's educational values. It might also be seen as one of the ways in which the head motivates children. It could also be an aspect of professional development for the child's teacher who was taking his or her first tentative steps in a new direction. This is less of a problem for individuals keeping a log for their own use than for the external researcher, who may well not be aware of the significance which the head attaches to particular activities. Nonetheless, it would be useful to record the purpose of the activity as well as the activity itself.

An alternative to the diary approach could be the use of a colleague as a critical friend who, on a reciprocal basis, would shadow the head for (say) a day. This would have the added advantage of providing an opportunity for discussion of how the two had used their time. Many heads experience headship as a lonely job yet do little to overcome their feelings of isolation by forming a network with other heads in their area. A review of how they use their time could provide a valuable focus for such a group.

2. *What needs doing?*

Having reviewed how one's time is actually being used, the next step is to review what tasks *need* to be done. In virtually any school, a comprehensive review of what needs to be done is almost certain to generate a depressingly long list of tasks which would require superhuman qualities to accomplish.

No heads are realistically going to be able to satisfy all the demands upon their time. It might therefore be a useful strategy to involve the whole teaching staff at this stage in the process. If they are fully aware of the impossibility of meeting all the demands and have had a voice in arranging the priorities, then they are less likely to be disappointed with the head's performance and, more importantly, more likely to be willing to take on tasks themselves. It is not at all unusual for teachers to have only a vague idea of what their headteacher actually does all day. After all, to the class teachers, who feel themselves to be under constant pressure from the demands of the children in their class all day, the head's position away from the stress of the classroom can sometimes seem enviable.

3. *How much of that can I delegate?*

If the staff have been brought into a discussion of the school's needs then the logical next step is the identification of areas of the head's activities which can be delegated. Delegation would leave the head more time to concentrate upon those activities which can be carried out only by a head and which are generally seen as important for the school.

Some of the tasks which heads undertake can be substantially reorganised in such a way that they almost disappear. I recall finding on my first day in a new headship that as headteacher of a large junior school I was responsible for issuing stock from a cupboard in the head's room. This led to an almost constant stream of interruptions as I handed out pencils, rubbers and paper. It was an easy matter to reorganise the stock so that teachers had access to whatever they needed, whenever they needed it. Unfortunately, not all management of time problems can be solved in such a simple and obvious way. The delegation problem is particularly acute for heads of small schools and yet, paradoxically, they are the ones who most need to delegate.

4. What priority do I attach to what remains?

The clear message from the research into how heads use their time was that they tended not to be very good at distinguishing between those problems which really *did* need their personal attention and those which did not.

There will always be an element of crisis management in every head's life. In real life it will never be possible to anticipate every crisis, and in most primary schools the head is the only person not wholly responsible for a class of children who is available to deal with unanticipated events. Frequently, if these crises are not dealt with speedily they become bigger and even more time-consuming. So the capacity to respond flexibly and quickly to an unanticipated event is, in fact, highly desirable. The unexpected parent complaining about a child's missing coat may seem like a tiresome interruption but, if there is no one available to reassure them that the school does take the problem seriously, the consequences can become disproportionately serious as the story spreads through the community. However, heads need to work out their priorities so that they do not respond to every problem as if it was just as important as every other.

5. How can I achieve a closer fit between what needs to be done by me and what I actually do?

The first piece of advice seems almost too obvious to need stating: do the most important things first. Given the realities of the job in a typical day – the fragmentation, the interruptions, the varied and unanticipated tasks – the chances are that, however well heads manage their time, they will not get much farther than the most important things.

An invaluable way of ensuring that time is spent first on what is most pressing and most important is to keep prioritised lists of things to be done: today, this week, this term, and this year. Crossing tasks off as they get done is particularly good for morale.

Finally it is important to monitor constantly how time is being used. From time to time, go through the first stage of this action guide again and keep another log. Several times a day pause and check whether it would matter at all if you did no do whatever it is you are engaged in. Surprisingly often, I found the answer was 'no', which only goes to show that, like so many of the managers in and out of school whose observed behaviour opened this chapter, I was a long way from making optimum use of the scarce resource of my time.

Action Guide for Optimising Use of Time

(1) What am I currently doing with my time? (Diary or log could help)
(2) What needs doing? (Bring staff into this discussion)
(3) How much of that can I delegate? (By cooperation not imposition)
(4) What priority do I attach to what remains?
(5) Achieve a closer fit between points 4 and 1 by:

- Doing the most important things first.
- Keeping prioritised lists to do
  ☐ today ☐ this week ☐ this term ☐ this year
  (Crossing them off as you do them is good for morale!)
- Constantly monitoring how you spend your time
  ☐ use another log ☐ would it matter if I didn't do this right now?

Further reading

There is a dearth of literature about the primary head's use of time. The papers referred to in the chapter are all worth reading in full but they may not be easy to find.

Hall, V. *et al.* (1986) *Headteachers at Work*. Milton Keynes: Open University Press. Although this book is focused upon secondary headteachers most primary heads would find it interesting and surprisingly relevant to their own work. It is based upon observation of fifteen heads for a day and four heads for a longer period.

Wolcott, H. F. (1973; reissued 1984) *The Man in the Principal's Office*. Prospect Heights, Illinois: Waveland Press. This study of one elementary school head has acquired the status of a classic. It portrays in detail the daily work life of 'Ed. Bell'. The book is very readable and is interesting to English heads because of the cultural contrast between their job and the more administrative post of elementary principal in the USA.

CHAPTER 7

Managing the Curriculum

Kenneth Baker is reputed to have said of the National Curriculum that it is an idea whose 'time has come'. As a history graduate he might have more accurately said that it is an idea whose 'time has come again'!

We did, of course, have a National Curriculum before, though last time around it was known as the Revised Code. This time it is up to heads and teachers to use their much higher level of professional skills to ensure that today's pupils do not suffer in the way that Victorian pupils suffered. It is said that those who do not know their own history are condemned to repeat it, so perhaps it is worth just reminding ourselves, briefly, of what happened last time.

The worst effects came not so much from the centrally defined curriculum as from the standards of attainment, and the tests to establish whether those standards had been reached. Only four years after the actual implementation of the Revised Code, the Chief Inspector, Matthew Arnold, noted the ill effects upon children's education:

> The mode of teaching in the primary schools has certainly fallen off in intelligence, spirit and inventiveness. . . . It could not well be otherwise. . . making two-thirds of the government grant depend upon a mechanical examination, inevitably gives a mechanical turn to the school teaching. . . more free play for the inspector, and more free play, in consequence, for the teacher is what is wanted. . . . In the game of mechanical contrivances the teacher will in the end beat us. . . .
>
> (Arnold, General Report for the Year 1867. Quoted in Maclure, 1965, p.81)

The present government's views about the purpose of the curriculum also have a déjà-vu air about them. Sir Keith Joseph, later echoed by Kenneth Baker in the consultation paper on the National Curriculum (DES, 1987), put it thus:

> It is vital that schools should always remember that preparation for working life is one of their principal functions. The economic stresses of our time and the pressures of international competition make it more necessary than ever before that Britain's work-force should possess the skills and attitudes, and display the understanding, the enterprise and adaptability that the pervasive impact of technological advance will increasingly demand.
>
> (DES, 1985, p.15)

Perhaps Sir Keith's bedside reading included old copies of Hansard for in 1870 W. E. Forster introduced his Education Bill thus:

> Upon the speedy provision of elementary education depends our economic prosperity... if we leave our work-folk any longer unskilled, notwithstanding their strong sinews and determined energy, they will become over-matched in the competition of the world.
>
> (Quoted in Maclure, 1965, p.104)

There is a fascinating story to be told of how we appear to be going round in a kind of helix on this matter of who controls the school curriculum. Suffice it to say, in this context, that the centralising tendency endorsed by James Callaghan in 1976 at Ruskin College has now borne fruit in the form of a National Curriculum which, ironically, Lord Callaghan voted against in the House of Lords. Even Kenneth Baker acknowledges his debt to Callaghan in his consultation document (DES, 1987, p.2). Most heads will have been practising teachers through this period of decreasing teacher control of the curriculum and, while they may look back fondly to the days when heads and teachers were left to decide both what to teach and how to teach it, there is little point in such nostalgia. Few are likely to be still in post by the time we work our way back round the helix! Meanwhile there is a challenging management task to do in ensuring that the curriculum is managed in a way which really does enable all our pupils to achieve their true potential.

A framework for managing the curriculum

The advent of the National Curriculum does not mean that the task of managing the curriculum has been removed from heads. Rather, the National Curriculum will impose certain mandatory parameters within which the curriculum will still have to be managed. This will become clearer if we look at a framework for managing the curriculum. The one which I plan to use is that devised by HMI and published as *The Curriculum from 5 to 16* as part of the 'Curriculum Matters' series (DES, 1985). Although this was written at a time when

Framework for Managing the Curriculum

1 *Educational aims*	
2 *Areas of learning and experience*	aesthetic and creative human and social linguistic and literary mathematical moral physical scientific spiritual technological
3 *Cross curricular issues*	environmental education health education information technology political education education in economic understanding preparation for the world of work careers education equal opportunities for boys and girls needs of ethnic minorities
4 *The elements of learning*	knowledge concepts skills attitudes
5 *The characteristics of the curriculum*	breadth balance relevance differentiation progression and continuity
6 *Assessment*	to improve pupils' performance to improve school's performance

Adapted from DES (1985) *The Curriculum from 5 to 16*. London: HMSO

the Government was still eschewing any legislative approach to the curriculum, it remains a useful management tool which still has relevance to the new situation. In addition to the booklet itself, I also intend to draw upon Richards' (1987) admirably clear exegesis of the booklet. On first publication *The Curriculum from 5 to 16* was largely ignored in many primary schools, its style was somewhat opaque and the framework was not readily visible. Richards has performed a valuable service for primary managers in drawing out the ways in which the ideas in the document may be used to manage the curriculum.

1. Educational aims

The first task for any school is to establish its aims, to decide what it is trying to achieve with its pupils.

This task is at one and the same time both deceptively simple and dauntingly complex. It is relatively easy for a school staff to reach a consensus on a statement of their aims which is couched in vague, general terms. The problems become apparent only when high-minded aspirations are translated into something which is more concrete and might actually serve as a guide to action.

Even a cursory look at primary school brochures reveals that schools find little difficulty in expressing their aims in the general sense, though few achieve the polished prose of the Warnock Report, which is quoted in *The Curriculum from 5 to 16*:

> . . . to enlarge a child's knowledge, experience and imaginative understanding and thus his awareness of moral values and capacity for enjoyment; and secondly, to enable him to enter the world after formal education is over as an active participant in society and a responsible contributor to it, capable of achieving as much independence as possible.
>
> (DES, 1978)

Quite what such a statement might mean in terms of the curriculum is by no means easy to see. It is capable of a wide range of interpretations and emphases and could therefore be used to justify a variety of practices. Probably the best way to view a general statement of aims is as a piece of symbolic rhetoric. Its function is to act as an integrating symbol which secures the broad support of teachers, parents and governors. This is not to say that it has no real value; on the contrary, the building of consensus on, and the presentation of, symbols which represent the value system of the school are key tasks for a head. Their importance for the ethos of the school and the projection of that ethos should not be underestimated. The problem comes when such aims are pressed into service for the rather different purpose of serving as educational objectives. The general aims need translating into more specific aims for each area of the curriculum. The National Curriculum attainment targets will provide specific behavioural objectives. The statutory requirements are likely to be the starting point for many schools which will want to go further in framing aims and objectives appropriate to their particular circumstances.

2. Areas of learning and experience

The National Curriculum used the traditional subject labels to define areas of learning. While this may represent a significant victory of the traditional (embodied in the politicians and the mandarins of Elizabeth House) over the 'edbizz' teachers and HMI, it is easy to exaggerate the importance of the label. In most cases it is a simple matter to equate the 'area of learning' with the 'subject':

HMI Curriculum 5–16		**National Curriculum**
mathematical	:	mathematics
scientific	:	combined sciences
physical	:	physical education
spiritual	:	religious education
human and social	:	history/geography history *or* geography
aesthetic and creative	:	art/music/drama/design
linguistic and literary	:	English
technological	:	technology

What does become apparent from such a pairing of terms is that the National Curriculum subject labels may gain marginally by being more widely understood by parents, but this is at the expense of a certain narrowness in the way that they conceive the curriculum. One should also remember that the National Curriculum does not have to be actually taught in subject packages. An integrated project is capable of covering a number of areas of study in a way that would meet the statutory obligations of the National Curriculum.

3. Cross curricular issues

HMI use this to cope with a range of topics that schools need to address without according them the status of separate areas of learning. These issues are what was sometimes referred to disparagingly as 'clutter in the curriculum' by those who hankered after a return to a more traditional curriculum. It is interesing to note their fate in the National Curriculum. The consultative document refers in passing to:

> ... a number of subjects or themes such as health education and use of information technology, which can be taught through other subjects. (DES, 1987)

One of the problems with this framework is that this category of 'cross curricular issues' tends to marginalise equal opportunities concerns, treating them as no more important than a variety of other issues. Yet in this area schools have statutory obligations to ensure that they do not discriminate on the grounds of race or gender. Additionally, many LEAs will have an equal opportunities policy which will also have to be observed. In view of this, most schools will want to pay special attention to this particular cross curricular issue when managing their curriculum. In most LEAs there will be members of the advisory service who will have a special responsibility for equal opportunities, and schools should regard them as a resource upon which they can draw when they are considering how best to ensure that they offer a curriculum that does not disadvantage children because of their race or gender.

4. The elements of learning

What is to be learned in relation to each area of learning? Each area of learning involves all four elements: knowledge, concepts, skills and attitudes. In developing schemes of work, all of these elements need to be considered in respect of each area. Thus these elements may be used to analyse what is, or should be, offered to each pupil.

5. The characteristics of the curriculum

These, too, offer a way of analysing a school's curriculum. They may be used both within each area of learning and across the curriculum as a whole.

- **Breadth** refers to the range of experiences offered and, for primary schools, raises the question of how far a single teacher can be expected to cover the whole range unaided. One solution here which is favoured by the Inspectorate is the use of curriculum leaders.
- **Balance** refers to the allocation of an appropriate amount of time and resources to each area and to each element of that area, so that children do not spend a disproportionate amount of time on, say, maths at the expense of linguistic and literary activities. Within the subject it would indicate the need to hold a balance between, say, oral and written language.
- **Relevance** refers to the need for the curriculum to relate and be seen to relate to the world in which the children live.
- **Differentiation** is closely connected with the idea of 'match'. The test here is one of appropriateness to each individual child's needs without losing breadth and balance. This is another point in the framework where it would be appropriate to ensure that the school's curriculum, as experienced by each child, provides for equality of opportunity.
- **Progression and continuity** are two inter-linked concepts. They refer to the desirability of children's learning moving smoothly forward, with each new piece of learning building upon what has gone before it. They therefore apply both within the school and between schools as children transfer from one phase of schooling to another. In the case of infant schools or departments, they also apply to liaison with nursery schools or pre-school playgroups. For children starting school for the first time there is a particular need to make and maintain contact with parents.

6. *Assessment*

Assessment refers to the need for the school to be continuously monitoring both the performance of its pupils and of itself. The statutory assessments at 7 and 11 will undoubtedly form part of any such monitoring system but on their own would be quite insufficient to meet either of the two purposes referred to above. Clearly, the results of any assessment system need to be recorded systematically in a readily usable form which can help the teacher match work appropriately for each child. A further requirement of any assessment and record keeping system is that it should be economical of teachers' and children's time. A form of profiling seems most likely to offer the compromise between time and usefulness. However, to meet the needs of the teachers who are going to use the profile, it would seem highly desirable that a school should devise its own system even if there is some slight loss as regards the minority of children who move from school to school.

This framework then offers an analytical tool which schools can use to monitor their management of the school's curriculum. The basic questions about the curriculum in any school have been arranged in a coherent form which facilitates the processes of curriculum review and development. The next question concerns the management structures which are necessary to ensure that those continuous processes do, in fact, take place.

Structures for managing the curriculum

Over the last decade or so the idea that teachers in primary schools should take responsibility for co-ordinating the work of the school in an area of the curriculum has gained currency. However, as Taylor (1986) shows, the idea that some teachers might have expertise or special skills in some area, and that these talents could be put to use, has been around for a great deal longer.

There are actually several ideas involved in this development which need disentangling if one is going to think clearly about what type of structure is likely to promote effective management of the curriculum.

Firstly, the range of the primary school curriculum has increased greatly since the days of the old elementary school when the class teacher system had its origin. No one teacher can now reasonably be expected to cover the whole curriculum with equal effectiveness without support. The support might consist of help and guidance from a colleague with a special knowledge of a particular subject. Alternatively, it might involve another teacher taking the class for a certain subject. Such arrangements were common, of course, for subjects like music or P.E. but much less so where they involved subjects which are more central to the class teacher's role, like maths or language.

Secondly, in many primary schools during the 1960s and 70s the atmosphere of curriculum freedom, with its stress on following the child's interests, led to a lack of planned continuity and progression between classes within the same school. This discontinuity was seen as a barrier to children's learning. Consequently, what was deemed necessary to remove the barrier was co-ordination of each area of the curriculum

Thirdly, successive Burnham pay agreements had made available a range of promoted posts of special responsibility which could be used for rewarding teachers who took on curricular responsibilities.

The first official document wholeheartedly to advocate some form of curriculum co-ordination was the HMI Primary Survey (DES, 1978). The inspectors observed that in about three quarters of schools teachers with special responsibility were having no noticeable influence on the quality of work in the school as a whole. Their observation concerning the other quarter was to resonate through the world of primary education as a model of good management practice:

> There was evidence in the survey that where a teacher with a special responsibility was able to exercise it through the planning and supervision of a programme of work, this was effective in raising the standards of work and the levels of expectation of what children were capable of doing.
>
> (DES, 1978, p.37)

This form of management structure, though now extended and separated from any necessary notion of additional salary, was endorsed by the House of Commons Select Committee on Education in their report entitled *Achievement in Primary Schools*:

> 9.18 We are of the view that it should be part of the ordinary duties of virtually every primary school teacher to act as a co-ordinator in some aspect of primary school work.
>
> (House of Commons, 1986)

They reached this conclusion based on the view that the range of the primary school curriculum was such that it was not reasonable for every teacher to cope unaided. They firmly rejected the alternative solution of specialist teaching, holding that the generalist class teacher system was more appropriate for primary age children. The committee also considered how a co-ordinator might operate:

> 9.25 We envisage that the colleagues giving help should do so in two main ways: by taking the lead in the formulation of a scheme of work; and by helping teachers individually to translate the scheme into classroom practice either through discussion or by helping in the teaching of the children. Much the most frequent method would be discussion.
>
> (House of Commons, 1986)

So clearly a collegial approach led by the head and the co-ordinator for that area of the curriculum is the preferred way for schools to manage the curriculum. There is a danger in this model that the school becomes inward looking. This need not necessarily be the case; amongst the co-ordinators' functions is that of keeping up to date with developments in their particular area. This involves attending courses, reading and then feeding this new information back into the school. The LEA will have advisory staff who have expertise in each area of the curriculum and they should be regarded as a resource which the school can call upon for help. Needless to say, the task is never accomplished; this is an ongoing activity, a constant process of evaluation and development.

Two recent studies (Campbell, 1985; Taylor, 1986) of how co-ordinators actually perform their roles both point, as did the Select Committee, to two particular problems which can impede them in being fully effective. The first, which Campbell sees as diminishing, is the acceptance of their advisory role by their colleagues. The Select Committee advocate a model in which teachers would turn to one another for advice in particular areas of the curriculum, so exchanging their roles of adviser and advised and thus avoiding any question of hierarchy. This view seems to rest upon an assumption that primary schools are operating upon a well developed collegial basis. It seems also to overlook the level of inter-personal skills that an effective co-ordinator needs. Campbell's view seems more realistic when he argues that pressure from HMI and others is gradually changing teachers' attitudes to seeking advice from colleagues.

The second barrier to effective co-ordination would be easier to overcome if the necessary funding were forthcoming. The barrier is that of shortage of time. Few co-ordinators actually received sufficient time free from their class teaching responsibilities to enable them to carry out their roles as co-ordinators. In the words of the Select Committee:

> 9.54 The inescapable conclusion we draw from this analysis is that primary schools cannot be expected to make much further improvement unless there are more teachers than registration classes.
>
> (House of Commons, 1986)

A problem for small schools?

The co-ordinator approach raises severe problems for small schools. Indeed, it threatens their very existence for it has provided one of the educational grounds for closing small schools. Every school needs sufficient children to have enough teachers for each of them to co-ordinate an area of the curriculum – so the argument runs. For example, *Better Schools* (DES, 1985) argues that the optimum size for a junior school is two form entry (8 teachers) and for a junior mixed and infant school, one form entry (7 teachers). Small schools, it is argued, could cooperate with each other in clusters to share expertise, or LEAs could provide additional support staff, perhaps in the form of advisory teachers. Many small schools are now doing just that, but it would be idle to pretend that co-ordination under such circumstances is an easy matter. Almost without exception, the heads and teachers from small schools that I have worked with on in-service training would claim that the other curriculum advantages which they enjoy outweigh the loss derived from the absence of a full set of curriculum co-ordinators. In other words, desirable though co-ordinators might be, their absence would certainly not justify the closure of small schools.

Managing the implementation of the National Curriculum

The National Curriculum will be gradually implemented, subject by subject, for successive age groups. As this happens, its implementation in the school will pose considerable management problems for heads and teachers, especially those with curriculum responsibilities.

Initially there is a whole new language to learn to use when talking about the curriculum. Such terms as programmes of study, statements of attainment, attainment targets, moderation, aggregation, norm-referencing and criterion-referencing will need to become part of teachers' everyday vocabulary when they are discussing the curriculum or the assessment of children.

The considerable problems of 'owning' something which has been imposed upon one should not be underestimated. Yet without a sense of commitment to the change, the best that can be hoped for is mere mechanical compliance. Mechanical compliance with the National Curriculum will undo decades of development of good primary practice and so it is imperative that heads find ways of avoiding such a retrograde outcome.

The proposals for Science (DES/Welsh Office, 1988) contain some grounds for optimism. It is quite clear that the Working Party have incorporated in their proposals recent ideas about good practice in this area of the curriculum. For many primary schools where science does not feature among their strengths, a programme of study along the lines proposed would be a welcome development.

The arrival of the National Curriculum means that an accommodation has to take place between the school's own curriculum guidelines and the required programme of study. A strategy is needed for achieving this in a way that is still to some degree consistent with the notion of teachers as professionals taking responsibility for the development of the curriculum of their school.

An incorporation strategy

One approach might be to do a content analysis and comparison between the programme of study and the school's guidelines noting:

- *Those items which appear in both the school's own guidelines and the National Curriculum programme of study.* Judging by the science proposals, this overlap is likely to be substantial.
- *Those items which appear only in the National Currriculum programme of study.* These must be added to the school's own guidelines and discussion should focus upon how that may be achieved.
- *Those items which appear only in the school's own guidelines.* In these cases discussion should focus upon whether they are still considered important by the staff and should therefore be retained, or whether they are now superfluous and should therefore be dropped.

It seems likely that most LEAs will produce a similar analysis of the content of their own LEA guidelines in relation to each programme of study. Any such comparison should be brought into the discussions about how to incorporate the statutory requirements into the school's curriculum.

Remember, too, that the National Curriculum does not dictate *how* the programmes of study should be taught. A wise strategy for minimising the ill effects of loss of control over content would be to focus discussion and development on pedagogy. The staff of a school still have a wide measure of autonomy in the workplace over how they organise their classes, so an emphasis upon how to teach the National Curriculum would probably be more productive of a positive climate than would a concentration upon that area where central control has been extended at the expense of the school.

Further reading

Campbell, R. J. (1985) *Developing the Primary School Curriculum.* London: Holt, Rinehart and Winston. This book discusses a wide range of curriculum issues in an analytical and comprehensive but very readable way. Special consideration is given to the way in which curriculum co-ordinators actually carry out their role in practice. The author advocates a 'collegial' approach to curriculum development which involves the whole staff of a school.

Taylor, P. (1986) *Expertise and the Primary School Teacher.* Windsor: NFER-Nelson. This book reports on a study of curriculum leaders in Birmingham, and contains many insights for the head seeking to implement an organisational structure based mainly on responsibility for areas of the curriculum.

CHAPTER 8

Managing Financial Resources

Traditionally, heads have directly controlled only a tiny proportion of the financial resources of their schools. In some Local Education Authorities (LEAs) this has already changed. In all others it is about to change for heads with more than 200 pupils on roll. Financial Delegation, Local Management of Schools (LMS) or, as it is more widely known, Local Financial Management (LFM) gives heads direct control of a far higher proportion of the school's total costs. Typically, a capitation scheme gives the head control of less than 4 per cent of the school's costs, while LFM gives control of nearer 90 per cent of the school budget to the head and Governors.

One cannot be precise about these figures because, amongst other reasons, practice in this area of school management differs considerably from authority to authority. In some LEAs, heads control little more than the school's budget for books, stationery, materials and communications. The Inner London Education Authority (ILEA) gave heads rather more control with its Alternative Use of Resources (AUR) scheme. This permitted virement – for switching a limited sum of money from 'say' staffing to capitation or vice versa. At the other end of the scale, Solihull, for example, gives heads control of all the major items of expenditure including staffing and internal maintenance.

To see this variety in context it might be helpful to think of schools occupying a place on a continuum of autonomy:

Degree of Autonomy for School

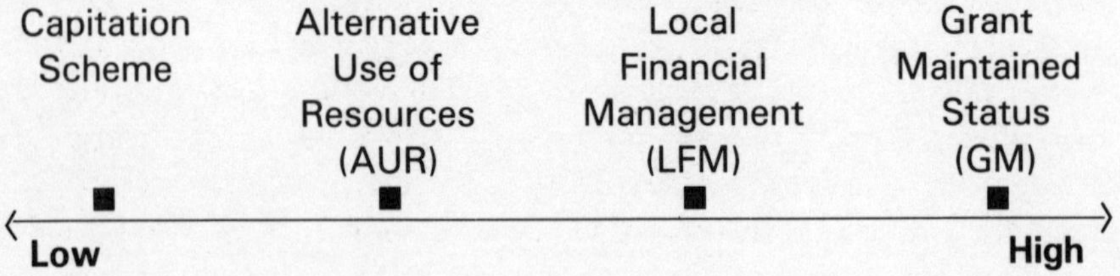

Capitation Scheme	Alternative Use of Resources (AUR)	Local Financial Management (LFM)	Grant Maintained Status (GM)
■	■	■	■

Low ← → **High**

Whatever position a school occupies on this scale of autonomy, the management task remains the same: to make the best possible use of the available resources in order to achieve the school's aims. What differs is the range of expenditure which the head can control in seeking to accomplish that task and, as a result, the room for manoeuvre which he has in allocating resources. Dependent in turn upon this, of course, is the sheer amount of work involved. The more autonomy a head has, then the more room for manoeuvre there is in taking decisions, and the more work there is involved. Autonomy raises far more issues than the workload, important though that might be, and I will return to these issues later in the chapter.

Primary school financial management is largely uncharted territory – there have been very few studies of how primary heads manage their financial resources. As Knight put it in his book *Managing School Finance*, which itself deals almost exclusively with secondary schools:

> Primary school costs are the 'Dark Continent' of school finance. (p.76) . . . we do not know very much about primary school costs at all . . . we know less about their costs than we know about the costs of our fish and chip shops.
>
> (Knight, 1983, p.99)

It could be that that situation will change with the advent of LFM and the requirement upon LEAs under the 1986 Education (No.2) Act Section 29, to make an annual financial statement of costs to the governors of every primary school. Currently, however, very little information is available.

How heads currently manage finances

Gray carried out a case-study of a primary school in 1984 (Gray, 1984) which revealed findings very similar to my own study of a primary school in the West Country (Hill, 1985). My own impression, and that of the many heads and teachers attending courses with whom I have shared the results, is that these findings are typical of the way that most heads on a capitation scheme manage their finances.

Current practice is characterised by two features: informality and secretiveness. Informality means that the assessment of needs and priorities within the school, and the evaluation of the effectiveness of resource use, were done informally by the head, with the actual ordering often delegated to a member of staff, often the Deputy Head. Secretiveness refers to the way that heads tended to keep financial information to themselves, leaving teachers in the dark about how much money was available or how the money was spent. Few teachers are fully involved in financial decision making.

Why do heads manage their financial resources in this way? Does it matter? Let us take the first question first. The whole culture of primary schools stresses informality. This informality pervades all the social relationships whether between teacher and child or between teacher and head. Informality derives in part from the small scale of most primary schools; 90 per cent of primary schools in England in 1987 had fewer than 300 pupils. It also derives from the high value placed upon informality as part of the child-centred ethos espoused by so many primary practitioners. An informal system of management thus fits well with the other aspects of life in a primary school.

The reasons for a secretive approach are a little more difficult to identify. It could be connected with the view that knowledge is power. The head is the only one in the school to know the overall situation. This enables him to behave in a micropolitical way. Competing demands from staff are more easily dealt with if none of the competitors knows for sure what the other demands are, nor knows the details of the school's budget. While this may be an accurate description of the way in which some heads behave, and while some may be very effective at manipulating the conflicting interests of their staff to achieve their own ends, it will hardly do as a prescription of how heads should effectively lead a team of professional teachers.

There may, of course, be a less sinister reason for heads failing to involve their staff fully in the financial affairs of the school. Many heads would claim that the amount of LEA money over which they have control is so small that they have virtually no room for manoeuvre and the decisions virtually take themselves. As the head in my case study pointed out:

> As far as criteria go for spending capitation it really is a question of when the scissors get rusty we have to get new ones and when the paint has gone we have to buy some more paint, when the paper has run out we have to buy more paper . . . it's just response to need. Teachers request certain things, so that will influence one, but really it's a question of *they* make the decisions when they consume the stock.
>
> (Hill, 1985, p.12)

If, as is the case in so many schools, 82 per cent of a meagre capitation allowance is being spent on consumable stock of the type referred to by this head, it hardly seems worth setting up time-consuming consultative procedures to discuss the allocation of finances: the potential savings are so miniscule and there are so many other matters upon which the time would be better spent. Under a capitation scheme, it would certainly seem sensible to share with the staff the information about how the school's money is spent and to invite comment and suggestions, but it hardly constitutes a major area of decision making for the school. It might be argued that the provisions of the Education (No.2) Act 1986, which require the production of a financial statement each year, mean that secretiveness is no longer an option for a head. However, these statements rarely include any detail about how the capitation allowance was actually spent.

If heads are currently not encouraging staff to participate in decision making about the capitation allowance because they do not regard it as an effective use of staff time due to the lack of scope for making decisions, then LFM may well change their view. When the school controls 90 per cent rather than 4 per cent of its budget then a rational, systematic and effective approach to making the decisions on that budget becomes essential. The view that decisions take themselves will be difficult to sustain. However, a recent study (Huckman, 1988) of a sample of primary schools in Cambridge which are involved in the county's LFM project shows that this need not necessarily be the case:

> There was little evidence to show that LFM had altered already existing patterns of decision making.
>
> (Huckman, 1988, p.140)

In this study the heads were found to be unlikely to share responsibilities with governors, teachers or even deputies.

Voluntary funds

Most of the flexibility which heads have under a capitation scheme comes not from control of LEA money but from the, sometimes, more substantial voluntary funds which a school raises for itself. Nationally, according to HMI (DES, 1987) 38 per cent of primary schools raised funds which exceeded 30 per cent of their capitation allowance. This figure hides some remarkable variations. The school which I studied raised voluntary funds equal to 120 per cent of capitation in a mainly middle class catchment area. The village school of which I was head regularly raised 250 per cent of capitation in a very deprived area (80 per cent free meals) because it was supported by the wider community. At the other end of the scale, HMI tell us that 28 per cent of primary schools raised a sum equivalent to less than 10 per cent of their capitation allowance.

Many heads feel a reluctance to spend time raising money for their school when there are so many other demands on their time. However, this attitude is often based on a false assumption and also ignores the beneficial side-effects of fund-raising activities. The false assumption is that it is necessarily the head who does the work. The head who regularly raises 120 per cent of capitation allowance is typical of those who raise large sums of money:

> Initially I spent a lot of time on money raising. But then it was able to be delegated – so it was. As soon as you have shown people what can be done you can delegate it . . . I resent any time spent on it because it diverts me from what I think I should be doing.
>
> (Hill, 1985, p.18)

In this school a teacher kept the accounts and the parents did all the other work involved in actually raising the money. My experience suggests that the schools which raise most money are the very ones where the heads personally spend little time doing it themselves but prefer to involve willing parents. Involving parents need not mean that the head and staff relinquish control of decisions on how to spend the money. There is certainly an increased need to account to parents for how the money is spent, but the vast majority of parents have no wish to be involved in the details of expenditure. However, most parents resent the 'extra' money which they have raised being spent on things which they regard as basic materials which should be provided by the LEA. This minor difficulty is usually easily resolved by careful allocation of expenditure on some items to one source of funds rather than to another.

Quite apart from the higher level of resourcing and increased flexibility which voluntary funds bring, the fund-raising events themselves can have other beneficial side-effects. Most of these have to do with raising the profile of the school in the community. Even a jumble sale brings people into the school building and while they are there displays can tell them about the work of the school. A Book Fair can raise money for the school while proselytising the cause of children's literature. A Summer Fair can help make the community more aware of its school. Raising money for the school provides parents with an opportunity to feel that they are involved with their child's school and that they are helping in a tangible way, even if they are not free to come into school during school hours to help in other ways in the classrooms. The danger to avoid is the obvious one of making people feel that the head always has a hand in other people's pockets!

In an ideal world a school would be provided with all its needs without having to raise money for itself; however such a utopia seems further away than ever. The most realistic response for a head would appear to be to encourage parents to raise money and ensure that every event has some ulterior motive in terms of presenting the school and its work in its community.

At the level of the school system there are understandable reservations about the gap which might open up between schools in wealthy, as opposed to poor, catchment areas. It would seem to be self-evidently true that a school's capacity to raise voluntary funds is linked with the level of incomes of the parents of children at the school. Thus the most deprived children will be likely to attend the least well resourced schools, the so-called 'Matthew Principle' – 'unto him that hath shall be given'. Such a situation would certainly call for some form of positive discrimination in favour of schools in low income areas. The ILEA used just such a deprivation index in calculating its payment of additional funds which were subject to its AUR scheme.

First-hand experience would suggest that the situation is not actually quite that simple. There are other powerful factors which affect a school's capacity to raise money and which are not related to the level of parents' incomes. Heads vary in their attitude to money-raising; some raise remarkably little in comfortable middle class catchment areas while others raise a great deal in areas which are poor. Some schools are able to reach the wider community within which they are located, raising money from people who do not currently have children at the school. Some schools attract support from commercial and industrial sponsors in their communities. Others have identified charities which pay out money for educational purposes. Some small schools combine to run events which would not be viable for each one on its own. In this area of the school's activities it seems once again as though the crucial factors are in the attitude and the behaviour of the head.

Local Financial Management (LFM)

Approximately 40 per cent of primary schools have a roll of 200+ and will therefore have a devolved budget under some form of Local Financial Management. Also, many LEAs are intending to exercise their option to extend LFM to smaller schools. These schemes will no doubt differ in detail from one LEA to another, in respect both of the range of expenditure items which are included in the school and of the administrative procedures to be adopted. Because these details differ in the pilot schemes and will differ in the statutory schemes, and because LEAs give detailed advice to schools about how to run their budgets, I do not propose to discuss the detailed administration of a devolved budget. However, many of the issues raised by the principle of LFM are common to all schemes and, as we shall see, are profound in their implications for the management of primary schools. Before Local Financial Management was imposed by the Education Act 1988, there was considerable debate about its desirability. Until the government made clear its intention to introduce LFM only a handful of LEAs had regarded it as worth trying, even on a pilot basis. The reason why is not hard to see. Local Financial Management involves handing over power and control to the heads and governors of schools, and thus involves a reduction in the power of the LEA to coordinate and control education within its area. Many heads were reluctant to take on the additional workload of LFM and risk attracting to themselves the odium attaching to the under-resourcing of schools. However, once an innovation becomes a statutory obligation heads will, for the sake of their pupils, try to make that innovation work in a way which maximises the advantages and minimises the disadvantages. In the case of LFM there are plenty of both: that is, plenty of pitfalls to avoid and plenty of gains to be won.

The rationale

Local Financial Management represents the application of the current orthodoxy in mainstream management theory to the management of schools. This holds that the most efficient form of organisation is to divide an enterprise into sub-units, set objectives for each unit, give the unit managers control of their own budget, and then measure their performance in achieving the set objectives. The strategy has already been applied to hospitals in the National Health Service following the Griffiths Report on NHS management. All hospital managers receive an allocation of resources within which they must take their own decisions on how best to achieve the objectives which are set for them. If it can work for people-processing units like hospitals, the argument runs, then why not for schools?

The Secretary of State commissioned a report on LFM from a private firm of management consultants, Coopers and Lybrand, who, not surprisingly, found enthusiastically in its favour and renamed it Local Management of Schools (LMS) to emphasise its extensive implications for schools and LEAs. Their report expresses the rationale for LFM in a very pure form, in language which educationists find alien:

> Good management requires the identification of management units for which objectives can be set and resources allocated; the unit is then required to manage itself within those resources in a way which seeks to achieve the objectives; the performance of the unit is monitored and the unit is held to account for its performance and for its use of funds. These concepts are just as applicable in the public sector as they are in the private sector.
>
> (Coopers and Lybrand, 1988, p.7)

The 'management unit' is the school, and the intention is that the LEA should set objectives which the head will then seek to achieve. The LEA will monitor the school's performance using 'performance indicators' such as exam passes, national benchmark test results and truancy rates.

A major defect of this attractively simple commercial solution to the problem of providing effective schooling is that the aims of education are both diverse and diffuse. Diverse, both in the sense that schools are trying to achieve a wide range of objectives and in the sense that there is by no means universal agreement about either the range of objectives or their relative importance. Developing creativity in children, for example, may feature highly in one school's aims and scarcely at all in another's. Spiritual development will be prominent amongst a Roman Catholic school's aims for its children but is likely to mean something rather different in an inner-city, multi-ethnic school. Not only are aims diverse but they are also diffuse in the sense that they are often necessarily vague and difficult to define. Consequently, they are slippery things when it comes to measurement. It has often been observed that the aims which are most susceptible of measurement are those which are least ambitious and have little to do with education as a life enhancing process. For example, it is a great deal easier to measure children's reading comprehension skill than to measure the extent to which reading has become an integral part of their life, bringing pleasure, intellectual stimulation, knowledge and an increased capacity to empathise with fellow human beings.

The Coopers and Lybrand report recognises that performance indicators can only measure some aspects of a school's performance and that they can be 'positively dangerous', but nonetheless it concludes:

> But conflict over the objectivity and applicability of performance measures should not be allowed to jeopardise the success of LMS.
>
> (Coopers and Lybrand, 1988, p.32)

This is an extraordinary conclusion in view of the report's earlier assertion that the whole scheme is predicated upon the setting of objectives and the unit's performance in achieving these objectives. The little difficulty of not being able to devise objective and applicable measures of performance is now being portrayed as a somewhat inconvenient feature of schools which must not be allowed to get in the way of applying a management system which is based on the very existence of such measures. If thinking of this quality was typical of educational management then educationists would be right to be suspicious of the rise of managerialism (Inglis, 1985).

There is another assumption built into the argument for Local Financial Management which is worth making explicit. Decisions, it is claimed by current management orthodoxy, are best made by those closest to the situation to which they apply. The most appropriate level for making decisions about a school's budget is that of the school. Thomas, who has been evaluating the Solihull scheme, points out that giving control of budgets to heads and governors assumes that they 'have a better view of pupil needs' than does the LEA, which currently controls the major part of the budget in most schools. He concludes:

> ... it is appropriate that we do not too readily take for granted the view that the resource decisions taken in schools are necessarily better than those taken outside schools by LEAs ... evidence of virement may indicate worse use of resources!
>
> (Thomas, 1987, p.4)

The relationship between most LEAs and most of their primary schools is such that the influence of the LEA upon practice in the school is likely to be benign and supportive. It is interesting that examples of widely admired primary practice have frequently occurred in particular LEAs or parts of LEAs. Thus Bristol was renowned for its early years provision, Leicestershire and Oxfordshire for the quality of their primary schools. In each case the standards in schools are traceable in some degree to the power and influence of certain key LEA officers and advisers: Parry in Bristol, Mason in Leicestershire, Moorhouse in Oxfordshire. Power over appointments, resources and in-service training budgets was an essential ingredient in their successful development of effective schools in their respective areas. It is unlikely that any LEA will ever again be able to affect practice in its primary schools in so direct a way. That, of course, is one of the objectives of the 1988 Education Act, but it is an objective based upon a determination to bring to heel a handful of so-called 'loony left' councils regardless of the effects on the other one hundred or so.

Opportunities for improved effectiveness

LFM certainly gives more power to the head. In the North American jargon LFM is about empowerment: the head teacher is empowered by being given control of over 90 per cent of the school's budget. Heads with powers of Local Financial Management will be in a better position to plan ahead because they will have control of the resources necessary for implementation instead of having to rely upon winning the support of the LEA. The school will be able to set its own priorities for expenditure in the light of its own perception of its needs, as they arise. The school will have an incentive to ensure that it obtains value for money. Money saved through careful checking of the price and quality of each of the services it buys will accrue to the school and be available for spending in ways decided by the school. Advocates of LFM also claim that it promotes the involvement of the governors, because at long last these 'sleeping partners' (Kogan, 1984) are given something worthwhile to do which increases their understanding of the school. However, to be involved in the school decision making processes in such a way would involve devoting considerably more time to the job of being a school governor than has hitherto been the custom. It may well be that there is a limited supply of selfless paragons.

In a similar way it is argued that LFM highlights the process of decision making within the school. Heads will be less able to be secretive about the budget if that budget covers 90 per cent of the school expenditure. Heads will encourage teacher participation in decision making on budgeting matters. Interestingly, Coopers and Lybrand speak of 'consultation' rather than 'participation' and stress that:

> It will be important to ensure that any such consultation does not unduly slow down decision-making nor reduce management flexibility.
> (Coopers and Lybrand,1988, p.34)

Certainly, from the point of view of head teachers anxious to enhance, rather than diminish, the professionality of their teachers, the emphasis should be upon encouraging participation in decision making rather than on maintaining their 'management flexibility'. Local financial management is an opportunity to increase teachers' involvement that should not be missed.

The research on school effectiveness shows the importance both of involving teachers in decision making (ILEA, 1986) and of there being a high degree of consensus among staff about school policy (Reid *et al.*

1987, p.29). Management of resources by the school itself will highlight the need to discuss and agree the aims of that school so that resources will be appropriately applied towards achieving those aims. Heads who involve their staff in those processes are therefore likely to be creating numerous benefits for the school in terms of its effectiveness. When seen from this angle Huckman's finding is all the more worrying:

> . . . the study also suggested that heads were unlikely to share responsibilities, even with their deputies . . . . In spite of the rhetoric of collegiality professed by all the heads in the study, in the area of decision making, they kept the reins firmly in their hands.
>
> (Huckman, 1988, p.140)

Pitfalls to avoid

The major danger for headteachers is that of being substantially diverted from their leadership role in the academic and pastoral life of the school into an administrative role concerned with the minutiae of running the school's budget. Again the lessons of the school effectiveness literature are clear: effective heads provide leadership in the academic and pastoral life of the school, setting standards of behaviour and achievement; less effective heads concentrate on smooth school administration (Leithwood and Montgomery, 1986, p.19).

There may well be a temptation when appointing staff to lay too much stress on the cost of a teacher, leading to the appointment of young staff with low qualifications. The savings achieved in this way can be considerable, with a gap of some £5,000 between the top and the bottom of the Main Professional Grade. Such evidence as there is in this area points to more experienced teachers being more effective.

Another temptation will be to exert undue pressure on non-teaching staff in the search for areas where costs be cut without directly affecting teachers and children. An example might be the reduction of cleaning hours without a reduction in expectations about the standard of cleanliness and hygiene in the school. Such a move would surely sour relationships with an important part of the school work-force. Similarly, a search for cost savings may lead to a shoddy standard of maintenance and decoration which would have long term cost implications for a future head.

Do heads have the necessary financial competence?

Undoubtedly, the biggest question of all concerns the heads' managerial competence: do heads have the necessary skills to ensure that Local Financial Management benefits their schools? The people best placed to pronounce on that topic are Her Majesty's Inspectorate of schools. In their annual reports on educational provision they comment directly on heads' management performance in the schools they have visited. The picture they painted in their 1987 report is not encouraging:

> ... unsatisfactory standards of provision are more often related to ineffective deployment of people and resources than to shortages of the resources themselves. (p.7)
>
> Deficiencies in the use of resources in schools were judged most often to be the result of inadequate perception of pupils' needs and poor management and deployment. (p.23)
>
> Inadequate management of resources by heads surfaced especially in the lack of clear criteria and consultation procedures for distributing capitation allowances.
>
> (DES, 1987, p.32)

As we move from a system which allowed heads to control 4 per cent of their school's budget into one where many will control 90 per cent of their budget, it is clear that heads are in need of training and advice. The problems of poor management under a capitation scheme noted by HMI are bad enough. It is essential that they are not vastly increased by the extra autonomy brought by Local Financial Management.

Further reading

Stenner, A. (1987) 'School-centred financial management'. In Craig, I. (ed.) *Primary School Management in Action*. London: Longman. A short but informative paper by a head from Cambridge about her experience of running a delegated budget. She is an enthusiastic advocate of LFM.

Caldwell, B. J. and Spinks, J. M. (1988) *The Self-Managing School*. Lewes: Falmer Press. These Australian authors advocate and explain a highly systematic approach to managing schools with devolved budgets. Its hyper-rational approach may not appeal to many English primary heads but their 'Collaborative School Management' system is adaptable to the more informal environment of the English primary school.

Downes, P. (ed.) (1988) *Local Financial Management in Schools*. Oxford: Blackwell. An interesting collection of papers some of which explain how LFM works while others, including another from Stenner, give different participants' experiences of operating a delegated budget.

CHAPTER 9

Managing Change

The management of change in the school is an area where the lessons accumulated from years of research into actual innovations can provide some real guidance for heads seeking to implement change. Much of the work has been done in organisations other than schools but still has relevance. Much of the work that has been done in schools comes from North America but, by allowing for the rather different educational practices of the USA and Canada, still has many insights to offer us into a complicated but central part of any head's job.

Michael Fullan, of the Ontario Institute for Studies in Education, has done more than any other single worker in this field to draw out the implications, for heads and administrators, of both his own and other people's research into the change process. In this chapter, I shall be making use of the insights which he offers and adapting them minimally where necessary to the context of the British primary school.

Most heads will have been around long enough to remember the Schools Council projects such as *Science 5 to 13* or even Nuffield Foundation projects like *Nuffield Primary Maths*. Initiating change in schools at that time meant gathering together a team of experts and getting them to research the field, write pilot materials, test them in a group of schools, revise them, test them again, then disseminate them to schools in general in the form of published curriculum materials. The materials were usually of a very high standard and contained, in the case of the two examples I have given, a wealth of ideas for teachers who were looking for ways of developing their classroom practice.

This approach to managing change is known as the 'Research, Development and Diffusion' (RD&D) approach (Havelock, 1971) and was widely used in this country and elsewhere during the 1960s and

1970s. The main problem came at the stage of getting that wider group of teachers in general to change their practice. Too often, even if heads bought the books, the books remained unopened and the ideas they contained unimplemented. The situation was rather different for the teachers who were involved in the pilot schools.

An object lesson

As a young teacher I worked in a school which was part of the Nuffield Primary Maths Project. Along with other teachers in the pilot schools I attended a Teachers' Centre one afternoon per week during the project, for supportive INSET provided by an enthusiastic tutor who also visited me in my classroom to give further help. The regular meetings at the Teachers' Centre also enabled the group of teachers to share their experiences and exchange ideas. The school received additional funds to buy the practical maths equipment needed to implement the new approach. The level of implementation of Nuffield Maths in that primary school was understandably higher than in schools which were not part of the pilot scheme.

What does research tell us?

If one looks at the 'state of the art' knowledge about how to manage change in schools it is intriguing to see how many of the recommended features were present in that pilot scheme in the late 1960s. Joyce and Showers (1980), for example, analysed the features of effective training for school improvement. They concluded that to be effective at actually inducing change in the classroom training should involve five components: presentation, demonstration, practice, feedback and coaching. These were all provided in the Nuffield Maths example. However, very rarely in my experience are sufficient resources made available to ensure that *all* of these components are present. Yet all too often we lament the fact that going on a course does not seem actually to alter teachers' behaviour in the classroom. It's the 'never mind the quality, feel the width' syndrome. Perhaps we would do better to have less quantity and more quality, to induce effective change in one or two schools than to give ineffectual training to so many teachers. Yet not all of Joyce and Showers' components need be expensive. If heads were aware that these components are *necessary* if the innovation is to be successful then they could ensure that the programme included them, even if that meant restricting the programme or pacing it differently.

What Makes Training Effective?

1 *Presentation of theory or description of skill or strategy* Readings, lectures, films and discussions are used to describe the new approach and its uses (INSET too often does no more than this)
2 *Demonstration of new approach* Through video or live demonstration with a class.
3 *Practice under simulated conditions* Trying out the new approach with a group of peers or part of a class.
4 *Feedback* Provision of information about performance given by peers, coaches or self.
5 *Coaching for application* Hands on, in-classroom assistance with the transfer of skills and strategies.

Adapted from Joyce and Showers (1980)

Planning a change

All change means more work and trouble in the early stages, even when it is a change which is designed to make things easier in some way. Changing means doing something differently from how you are doing it right now, and that means more work. The longer you have been doing something in a particular way, the easier you are likely to find it to continue doing it that way. The new way can be threatening; after all, you have probably got quite good at doing it the old way and you may not be so good at doing it this new way. So why change?

There needs to be a convincing answer to this apparently simple question. A number are possible and they tend to vary in their power to convince. Firstly, one can use naked power and simply command that a change shall take place, using incentives or sanctions to ensure that it does. This is what Bennis, Benne and Chin (1969) called a 'power-coercive' strategy. Not surprisingly, it rarely generates any sense of enthusiasm amongst the coerced and so it usually produces little more than compliance. Secondly one can assume that one's colleagues are rational and use the power of argument to convince them that the proposed change is both desirable and effective. This is an 'empirical-rational' strategy and, while it may be an essential ingredient, it is rarely sufficient on its own, as Joyce and Showers (1980) showed. The third strategy is labelled 'normative-re-educative' by Bennis, Benne and Chin. This strategy seeks to change the attitudes and beliefs, and thereby the behaviour, of the teachers. It stresses that changing involves learning to do something new. The most effective strategy is this third approach of changing the norms of the group, although it needs to be underpinned by a strong rational case for change.

If the head can establish a climate within the school such that the performance of each teacher, of the head him/herself and of the school corporately are seen as capable of continuous improvement, then change directed towards school improvement will be more likely to succeed.

Loucks-Horsley and Hergert, who have both been involved in facilitating change in American schools, have produced a seven-step action guide to managing change for school improvement. It is based upon moving the school from 'Our school as it is now' towards 'Our school as we'd like it to be':

A Seven Step Action Guide

Step 1: Establishing the school improvement project.
Step 2: Assessment and goal setting.
Step 3: Identifying an ideal solution.
Step 4: Preparing for implementation.
Step 5: Implementing.
Step 6: Review.
Step 7: Maintenance and institutionalisation.

Source: Loucks-Horsley and Hergert (1985)

How to implement change

Fullan (1982a) has produced a set of ten principles of effective change which are derived from recent research into the change process in schools. The old RD&D approach does not embody many of these ten principles except in the case of the pilot schools which were involved in the development of the new materials. A further very fundamental problem of initiating change using the RD&D approach is that the materials may have been superb but they were not the result of teachers attempting to solve a problem which was confronting them in their classrooms. As Goodlad (1976) memorably put it they '. . . turned out to be answers in search of problems.'

Fullan's Ten Principles of Effective Change

1. *Implementation is a process not an event* – it is a learning process which occurs gradually over time.
2. *The innovation will get adapted* – this may be good or bad but it is going to happen anyway.
3. *Implementation is a process of professional development and growth* – it is both personal (the individual teacher changes) and social (change is a resocialisation process).
4. *Implementation is a process of clarification* – as users come to understand the change in materials, behaviour and thinking.
5. *Interaction and technical assistance are essential* – regular opportunities for interaction, mutual help and external assistance must be provided.
6. *Planning at the school and system levels is a necessity* – if the many naturally occurring obstacles to implementation are to be overcome.
7. *Plans must address the three aspects of change and monitor progress during implementation* – i.e. materials, teaching approaches and thinking.
8. *Developing and using a plan is itself an implementation problem* – people must learn to use it and modify it.
9. *One hundred per cent implementation is probably not desirable and in any case is impossible* – a plan is effective if its outcomes are better than previous plans or left to chance, no plan will ever solve all the problems.
10. *The ultimate goal of implementation is not to implement X or Y but to develop the capacity for schools and individuals to process all innovations* – implementation of any specific innovation will get easier as schools develop their basic capacity for change.

Adapted from Fullan (1982a)

In the same paper Fullan considers twelve factors which affect implementation, from which I wish to highlight five which relate to the characteristics of the innovation and of the school. The other seven relate to characteristics of the LEA and of the national system. These five, however, lie at least partly within the control of the school itself and are therefore worthy of special consideration:

Factors Which Affect Implementation

Characteristics of the innovation

(i) *Need* for the change – is the need recognised, is this innovation perceived as the answer to that need?
(ii) *Clarity/complexity* of the change – are teachers clear about what they are actually to do, how complex is the innovation? The more complex and unclear, the more likely that the change will be avoided.
(iii) *Quality and availability of materials* – are adequately developed, high quality materials available in the school?

Characteristics of the school

(i) *The headteacher's actions* – does the head play a direct active role in leading the process of change?
(ii) *Teacher/teacher relations and actions* – is provision made for the teachers to assist each other in addressing and resolving the problems raised during implementation?

Adapted from Fullan (1982a)

The head's role in the management of change is crucial. Changes which have the active support of the head are more likely to succeed than those that do not. The question is, what form should this active support take?

> A large percentage of principals (at least half) operate mainly as administrators and as ad hoc crisis managers. These principals are not effective in helping to bring about changes in their schools. Those principals who do become involved in change do so either as direct instructional leaders or as facilitative instructional leaders. Both styles of leadership can be effective.
>
> (Fullan, 1982b)

Some heads, then, are effective because they are actually involved in the teaching of a particular area of the curriculum and provide a direct form of leadership in the actual teaching. Others are effective by facilitating the implementation of changes by others. This they may do by providing resources or by making suitable administrative arrangements, but most of all they do it by setting a climate in the school which fosters continuous improvement.

The role of the head in managing change

Weindling and Earley's (1987) study of newly appointed secondary heads found that teachers, far from resisting change, expected new heads to make changes. In this study most of the innovations originated with the head rather than from outside the school or from elsewhere within the school. Most of the changes were initiated by new heads. A comparison group of 'old' heads, with from three to eight years experience, introduced very few changes. Whether this reflects the fact that they already had their innovations in place or that they had lost momentum is not clear.

The early changes which heads introduced tended to be in the areas of improving communication and consultation within the school and of promoting the school's image. Internal communications were most frequently improved by introducing staff briefings, holding more staff meetings and issuing weekly bulletins. The measures introduced to improve the school's image were more wide-ranging but included: improved liaison with feeder primary schools, introducing uniform, securing building improvements, publishing newsletters for parents and pupils, redesigning pupil progress reports for parents and establishing links with local press and community groups. Curriculum changes take longer to implement but in this area new heads were likely to initiate reviews of the curriculum at an early stage. Although all of these findings relate to secondary heads, it seems likely that the changes made by new primary heads are very similar.

The timing or pacing of change was an aspect of the management of change that caused the new secondary heads some difficulties. The usual advice given to heads on appointment is to 'make haste slowly', to take time to evaluate the school before introducing changes. The *Junior School Project* new heads reflected this advice when they stressed that they '. . . tried not to make too many changes too quickly.' (ILEA, 1986, p.37) However, given that the teachers have an expectation of change when a new head is appointed, it is possible to miss the opportunity for change that this affords. Getting the timing right is not simply a matter of going slowly. In four schools out of sixteen in Weindling and Earley's study, the overall teacher attitude to the heads' changes was negative. In two schools the teachers thought the head had introduced change too quickly but in the other two they felt that the pace of change had been too slow. In these four cases the heads had clearly failed to read the situation correctly and match the pace of change to the circumstances in which they found themselves.

A related pitfall for new heads seeking to introduce changes is that it is all too easy to fail to give sufficient credit for what the school is already doing well. An emphasis on change can be seen by the teachers as an implication that the school is generally deficient. Such a message, however unintentionally transmitted, will not create an atmosphere conducive to mutual trust in which learning can be shared.

It is the creation of just such a climate in the school which is the key part of the head's leadership role in the management of change. A climate which supports the continual quest for improvement will be one in which all of the teachers will see their teaching performance as something to be continuously monitored, reflected upon individually and collectively, and improved.

The head as the facilitator of change

The head's facilitating role is important throughout the innovation process. Indeed, insofar as he or she has set a climate which promotes school improvement as a continuous process, the role actually precedes the change process. However the head's facilitating role is particularly important during the implementation phase. In most primary schools the head is the only member of staff with the opportunity to see what is happening in the classrooms while work is actually in progress.

When Peters and Waterman (1983) studied the management of America's top performing companies, they discovered that effective managers used a technique which Peters and Waterman dubbed 'Management by Wandering Around' (MBWA). Now that it has a name, we can recognise that effective primary heads also make extensive use of MBWA! There is perhaps no more important time to use MBWA than during the implementation phase of the change process. Loucks-Horsley and Hergert advocate MBWA and have produced a list.

Some Things to Look For While Wandering Around

- Use or non-use of new practices and materials
- Successful implementors
- Teachers having trouble, and what the trouble is
- Complaints and negative remarks, informal or voiced as jokes
- Logistical problems; for instance, paper shortages, storage problems, needs for new kinds of space or equipment
- Classroom management problems
- Teacher developed techniques that work

Source: Loucks-Horsley and Hergert (1985)

Coping with nationally-initiated change.

There is a strong tradition in this country of change being initiated at the classroom or school level in response to a problem that teachers have encountered in their work. In the wake of the 1988 Act, schools are facing a rather different type of change: nationally initiated change which has its origins outside the school. Nor is it only the source of the change that is different: the order of magnitude of the change expected of teachers is without precedent.

It must be tempting for a Secretary of State to declare that change will take place in classrooms throughout the country on a certain date. The chances of such an approach actually achieving real change are very slim. Achieving real change in schools is a time-consuming process of resocialisation which is unlikely to be brought about simply by legislation. The auguries from the accumulated evidence about the management of change suggest that a power-coercive approach will secure not much more than mechanical compliance from those who have been coerced into changing. The changes will be adapted and schools will tend to erect a facade of change while continuing to function largely as they have done in the past. It is a great deal easier to change the structure of education by legislation than it is to change its content and quality.

There is a school of thought which says that none of this matters a great deal. The 1988 Act will have served its political purpose if the facade changes. The government will have been seen to have acted and that was the primary purpose of the Education Reform Act. Be that as it may, the problem with this analysis from the point of view of those working in schools is that they are still left with the problem of making the changes work for the sake of the children. So, whatever the political argument might be about the 'real' intentions of the politicians, for heads the question will be: 'How can I implement these required changes in a way that enhances the quality of education that the children receive?'

There is a shred of evidence from the USA (Huberman and Miles, 1984) that imposed change can succeed under certain conditions. Huberman and Miles examined the change process closely over a period of three years in twelve schools in the USA, as one part of a massive research project which studied federal school improvement programmes affecting 146 school districts. Their findings have suddenly acquired a special relevance for educators in this country now that we have entered an era in which change is centrally conceived and centrally imposed. Huberman and Miles are unequivocal in their findings: centrally imposed change can work but not if pressure alone is used. Pressure to change must be accompanied by steps which ensure both that teachers have the necessary skills to carry out the change in the classroom and that they have the necessary commitment to make the change work. This requires a steady flow of support. The pressure needs to be exercised in a context of 'teacher–administrator harmony' in such a way that it is perceived as firm rather than tyrannical:

> Administrative pressure without support and commitment simply leads to teacher resistance and failure; user influence over implementation without commitment to the spirit of the innovation leads to blunting or downsizing. (p.279)
> Large-scale, change-bearing innovations lived or died by the amount and quality of assistance that their users received once the change process was under way. (p.273)
>
> (Huberman and Miles, 1984)

Much of the responsibility for providing such assistance lies primarily with central government and to a lesser degree with local education authorities, as Huberman and Miles point out:

> One of the clearly important adjuncts of the decision to go the ambitious route is *sustained assistance*; without it, large-scale programs will simply backfire or wither.
>
> (Huberman and Miles, 1984, p.280)

However, heads still have some scope for ensuring through the staff development programme that appropriate assistance is given to their staff in implementing the National Curriculum, the new assessment procedures and Local Financial Management. We know from work like that of Huberman and Miles that this assistance is vital if these changes are to enhance the quality of education that the childen are to receive. Heads also have a responsibility to generate commitment to the changes for exactly the same reason. Probably the soundest strategy for doing this is to present the changes as developments of current school policies. Thus, for example, the school which already has a commitment to curriculum development will still be involved in developing its curriculum, even though it now has the word 'national' in front of it. Or in the case of assessment, few teachers would dispute the contention that they should match the work to the needs of the child, thus assessment in the new prescribed ways can be seen as a development which aids the process of matching. Viewed in this way, Local Financial Management is simply a logical extension of the range of decision making over which the school has direct control and in which the staff may participate.

In a very real sense it is the head who is caught in the middle of what is for some an unenviable moral dilemma. On the one hand, heads are committed to the children in their school and to offering them the best possible education; while on the other hand, there may well be elements of the changes they are required to implement about which they have deep reservations.

In some ways nationally-initiated change is just like home-grown change except that it is much more difficult to make work successfully. Its greater difficulty is due to the very fact that it is not home-grown. Its origins do not lie in the efforts of a group of professionals seeking an answer to a problem or a better way of doing part of their job. The group therefore has no sense of ownership of the change and hence lacks the same degree of motivation to make it succeed.

The major challenge for heads will lie largely in generating a commitment to the changes on the part of their staff. The key to doing this seems to lie in viewing the changes from the perspective of school improvement. Such an approach would seek to adapt the changes as far as possible to the particular circumstances of the school, with the aim of improving the school rather than simply of complying with the law. Clearly this approach will be a great deal more feasible in a school where the head has established a climate of mutual trust in which the performance of the school is continuously monitored, reviewed and developed.

Further reading

Fullan, M. G. (1986) 'The Management of Change'. In Hoyle, E. and McMahon, A. (eds.) *The Management of Schools*, London: Kogan Page. This may be only a short paper of some twelve pages but it contains a wealth of insights derived from the author's extensive knowledge and experience of managing change. His style is clear and direct.

Nicholls, A. (1983) *Managing Educational Innovations*. London: Harper and Row. This is an admirably clear overview of the whole topic and includes a chapter which deals with the head's role as a manager of change.

Huberman, A. M. and Miles, M. B. (1984) *Innovation Up Close: How School Improvement Works*. New York: Plenum Press. This book examine closely the implementation of change in schools. Although it originates in the USA its focus upon externally initiated change makes it especially relevant to an English head. The authors show clearly the conditions that are required for centrally imposed change to work at the school level. The book is written in a style which holds the reader's attention to the last page.

CHAPTER 10

Managing for Continuity

First schools, infant schools, junior schools, junior mixed and infant schools, and some middle schools are all forms of primary school catering for different age groups of children. All of them pass their pupils on to other schools at varying ages. In all of these schools the management challenge for the headteacher is to ensure that the change from one school to another does not cause disruption to the children's learning and development. This applies equally whether the school is receiving pupils or sending them on to another school.

Each summer children leave primary schools at the ages of seven, eight, nine, ten, eleven and twelve, depending on the structure of primary schooling in the area of the country in which they live. Some of the four and five-year-old entrants will have attended a nursery school and so they too will be involved in changing school. Viewed in this way, it is only six-year-old children who are not involved in changing school somewhere in the country. In spite of the extra complexity brought about by the introduction of first and middle schools, eleven is still the most common age for children to change school, as the table shows.

Because eleven remains the most common age for transfer, the larger part of this chapter relates to changing school at that age. However much is equally applicable to the transfer of children from first to middle schools or from infant to junior schools. Indeed, much is also applicable to the transfer of children from infant to junior departments within the same junior mixed and infant (J M & I) school. In fact, some of the most interesting research on children changing school to which I shall refer was carried out in authorities which have some form of middle schooling.

Eleven became established as the 'proper' age of transfer from

Full-Time Pupils in Maintained Primary Schools: January 1987

Infants	475,202	13%
First	430,931	12%
Junior & infants	1,808,245	50%
First & middle	102,717	3%
Junior	610,032	17%
English as second language centres	1,003	0.03%
Middle deemed primary	148,808	4%
Total primary	3,576,938	100%

Source: DES Statistics, 1987, Table A4/87

primary to secondary schooling with the Hadow Report of 1926 on *The Education of the Adolescent*. In the manner of such committees of enquiry, they sought what was considered to be the best-informed advice of the period and found a consensus, which is exemplified in this reference to the evidence of Nunn:

> . . . Professor T. Percy Nunn informed us that he had long been in favour of a 'clean cut' across our public educational system at the age of 11 plus.
>
> (Board of Education, 1926)

By 1931 the subsequent Hadow Report on primary education was laying more stress on continuity:

> It is true indeed that the process of education from the age of five to the end of the secondary stage should be envisaged as a coherent whole, that there should be no sharp division between infant, 'junior' and post primary stages and that the transition from any one stage to the succeeding stage should be as smooth and gradual as possible.
>
> (Board of Education, 1931)

So, no sooner was eleven established as the age for transfer than the need for arrangements to minimise the resulting disruption was recognised. Successive official reports and publications from 1931 until the present day have drawn attention to the desirability of continuity. The Plowden Report (CACE, 1967) has an entire chapter entitled 'Continuity and Consistency between the Stages of Education.' HMI in *The Curriculum from 5 to 16* (DES, 1985) included continuity as one of the criteria by which the curriculum should be judged. *Better Schools*

(DES, 1985) exhorted schools and LEAs to take steps to improve continuity between schools:

> The 5–16 curriculum needs to be constructed and delivered as a continuous and coherent whole, in which the primary phase prepares for the secondary phase, and the latter builds on the former.
>
> (DES, 1985, p.21)

There are several issues intertwined in the debate about continuity. Few schools would dispute the need for arrangements which smooth the path of *transition* from one school to another for children who are inevitably involved in a process of adjustment. In order to reduce the problems experienced by the children and by the receiving school, most schools have arrangements for *liaison* procedures. Liaison may make transition less fraught for children, their families and the new school, but it does not necessarily involve any continuity. *Continuity* refers most frequently to the curriculum and sometimes to pedagogy, and involves agreement between schools from different phases about aims and objectives; content; skills and teaching methods.

Schools in general find it easy to agree upon liaison procedures to facilitate adjustment by the children as they move to their new school. After all, it is not in the interests of either school to have worried and anxious parents and children, if that can be avoided or at least minimised. Continuity in terms of what is taught has proved much more difficult to achieve. However, the arrival of the National Curriculum which applies from five to sixteen will impose a more continuous curriculum where voluntary efforts had largely failed. Continuity in *how* children are taught is likely to remain elusive. Much of the difficulty in achieving continuity of pedagogy has its orgin in the ignorance and misunderstanding which each phase has about the other.

Across the great divide?

The interface between primary and secondary schooling throws the differences, or supposed differences, into sharp relief. The differences may be in pedagogy, curriculum and general organisation or ethos. The stereotyped image of primary and secondary school teachers is reflected in the oft-repeated story that if you ask secondary teachers what they teach they will say ‘French’ or ‘physics’ or ‘history’. Ask primary teachers the same question and they will answer ‘children’.

For secondary teachers their subject allegiance can be an important part of their identity as a teacher. Their claim to professional status rests on a claim to have mastered an academic discipline, and most will have a degree in that subject to prove their claim. Their professional training as teachers is normally only one third of the length of their training in their subject. Primary teachers, on the other hand, rarely have degrees in a particular subject and will have spent a large part of their time in Higher Education training as teachers. Their claim to professional status rests on their knowledge of teaching. It is significant that the primary teacher's claim is generally perceived, even within the profession, to be weaker. The status of the primary teacher's expertise is lower.

The stereotype of the secondary teacher's classroom performance is of a didactic instructional style delivered from the front of the classroom. The stereotype of the primary teacher at work is of someone leading from the rear – moving around the classroom assisting groups of children or individuals working on a variety of activities deriving from the children's own interests. Like all stereotypes, this picture is far from accurate.

Many primary teachers are not as child-centred as the stereotype portrays them. True, the majority of classrooms are arranged informally in groups and have been for the best part of two decades. What actually happens within those informally arranged classrooms fits rather less well with the stereotype. Bealing (1972) came to the following conclusion from surveying the practice of a large number of junior teachers:

> Despite the relatively informal classroom layouts adopted by the vast majority of teachers there was so much evidence of tight teacher control over such matters as where children sit and move that it seems highly doubtful that there is much opportunity for children to choose or organise their own activity in most classrooms.
>
> (Bealing, 1972)

When HMI reported the results of their survey of primary education they revealed that fewer than one in twenty teachers used a 'mainly exploratory' approach whereas about three-quarters used a 'mainly didactic' teaching style. Later studies by various authors (e.g. Galton *et al.*, 1980; Boydell, 1980; Barker Lunn, 1982 and 1984) all show a similar picture with the trend being away from the 'child-centred' Plowden approach:

> We find on the contrary, that primary schools concentrate very heavily on basic number and language work, with a particularly strong focus on writing (normally copying from books, work-cards or from the blackboard).
>
> (Galton *et al.*, 1980)

The picture painted by this evidence is clearly quite different from, and a great deal less flattering than, that painted by the stereotype. The unflattering stereotype of secondary schooling is likewise far from accurate. Many secondary schools have made great efforts to use some of the more active learning approaches more often associated with the best primary practice.

The ethos or atmosphere of the two phases is also held to be different. In part this derives from the 'child-centred' or 'subject-centred' distinction caricatured in the stereotypes. This distinction is somewhat dubious to say the least, as we have seen. The secondary school is certainly different in some of its organisational features and this difference has consequences for the pupils. Firstly, and most obviously, the average secondary school is much larger than the average primary school. In 1987 just under 90 per cent of all primary schools had fewer than 300 pupils on roll whereas over 90 per cent of secondary schools had more than 300 pupils. A second organisational feature is also markedly different: the number of teachers that a pupil encounters. In the vast majority of primary schools pupils have one class teacher with whom they have close and continuous contact for most of their day; whereas in most secondary schools pupils will meet a multiplicity of teachers, normally a different teacher for each subject. The nature of the relationship between pupil and teacher inevitably differs as a result. Nor should one lose sight of the fact that a secondary school contains older children who have different interests, a greater involvement in their peer culture, and a less pliant attitude towards the school and its regime. All of these features combine to produce a social world within the school which differs significantly from primary to secondary. Also, each of these features crops up, as we shall see, on the lists of worries which primary children have as they prepare to leave the primary school.

Why promote continuity?

This might seem like one of those questions whose answer is so obvious that there is little point in posing it. However, there are those who, like Sir Percy Nunn some sixty years ago, still advocate a 'clean cut' or – to put it more technically and therefore perhaps more acceptably – intentional discontinuity. This argument points out the advantage to some pupils of starting with a 'clean slate', of the stimulus of new teachers with different teaching methods and of the excitement of being in a new, larger environment with older children. Nor should one completely dismiss this point of view, because the move to secondary school can be a stimulus in some or all of those ways. The argument for continuity is not an argument for making secondary schools just like primary schools, rather it is an argument for avoiding unnecessary disruption in children's learning and development.

Galton's ORACLE studies provide clear evidence of the ill effects to children's learning of the transfer as currently handled:

> ... nearly 40 per cent of pupils scored less on the same tests of basic skills in the June following transfer than they did in the final term in the old school.
>
> (Galton and Willcocks, 1983, p.169)

Heads and teachers seek continuity within the school in order to achieve progression in the work of their pupils and since there is no magical change in those pupils during the summer holiday there can be no good reason for an artificial break in their learning. The Bullock Report on language development had no doubts on this topic:

> We have urged that reading be regarded as a continuously developing skill and that language be extended to meet increasingly complex demands as the child grows older. Neither aim can be achieved without close cooperation.
>
> (DES, 1975)

The Cockcroft Report on the teaching of mathematics produced this graphic description of the consequences for the child of discontinuity:

> If a pupil is suddenly expected to attempt work which is beyond his capacity or finds himself bored at the outset by having to repeat work he has already mastered ... his mathematical development [is] interrupted.
>
> (DES, 1982)

HMI in their discussion document on the whole curriculum during the statutory years of schooling were unequivocal:

> The main points at which progression is endangered by discontinuity are those at which pupils change schools; they also include those at which children enter school, change classes or teachers ... curricular planning ... between schools should aim to ensure continuity.
>
> (DES, 1985, p.48)

In spite of this widely recognised need for more continuity the evidence suggests that little has actually been achieved. The HMI Primary Survey (DES, 1978) found that 29 per cent of schools regularly held discussions on continuity. Even this low figure may be misleading. It is perfectly possible to hold such discussions without actually changing anything. Stillman and Maychell (1984), like Galton and Willcocks (1983), found no evidence of curriculum continuity. HMI shared this view:

> On the whole, schools have been more successful at these transfer points in looking after the pastoral welfare of pupils than in achieving curriculum continuity.
>
> (DES, 1985, p.50)

Why is continuity so difficult?

Given that the official rhetoric since 1931 has been so strongly in favour of continuity, and given that most schools make some effort to smooth transition, why is it that so little has been achieved on the continuity front?

Stillman and Maychell's study of school transfer on the Isle of Wight devoted considerable attention to this topic. Their interviewees expressed reasons why curriculum continuity could not work yet none of these seemed to be insuperable problems:

> . . . other reasons must be sought to explain this reluctance. Our observations would suggest there are three major influences which make it difficult for teachers to enter into inter-sector continuity discussions: attitudes generated by sector hierarchy, poor experience of the 'other' sector, and professional isolation.
>
> (Stillman and Maychell, 1984)

Status hierarchy bedevils the English education system. For illogical reasons status depends on the age and ability of the children one teaches. Probably the most professionally demanding teaching I have ever done was when I had a class of six-year-olds, yet teaching infants is still seen by many both inside and outside of the profession as a low status occupation. Even the Registrar General in his classification of occupations promoted me to Social Class I when I transferred to teaching in a university. Sector hierarchy not only leads to secondary teachers looking down on their primary colleagues but also, as a concomitant, leads to primary heads being unduly sensitive to perceived direction from 'above'. This generates an atmosphere in which the mutual trust and confidence necessary for developing continuity are lacking.

Given the lack of first hand knowledge of the 'other' phase and the isolation in which many teachers work, the stereotypes outlined earlier are available to fill the gap. Yet we know that those stereotypes are misleading. Nash (1973) found that primary teachers were passing on to their pupils their own misconceptions about secondary schools. This was a phenomenon which the ORACLE team also noted:

> A common view of transition is that it marks the stage where the excitement of learning ends and the grind begins. In the ORACLE study we found that, towards the end of the final year, many teachers 'topped up in basics' and warned the children that 'you won't get away with work like that up there'.
>
> (Galton, 1983, p.6)

Secondary teachers too were operating with their new pupils with a faulty and misleading view of primary education which led them to set work which was poorly matched to the children's needs. Galton tells a vivid story of an instance of this which he observed:

> In the final term before transfer the children gave the [ORACLE] observers a farewell lunch. They planned the menu, went out and bought the food, cooked and served it in splendid fashion. The menu consisted of French onion soup, followed by spaghetti bolognaise, followed by apple tart and custard with coffee and mints to follow. The same children were observed during their first cookery lesson after transfer preparing . . . cheese on toast and making a cup of tea. Even with this simple task the children only got round to cooking after a considerable amount of note taking!
>
> (Galton, 1983, p.6)

The child's eye view of transfer

Every teacher of fourth year juniors knows, as do most parents of children due to change school, that many children are anxious about changing school. When one considers that for an adult a change of job is well recognised as a stressful incident, then no one should be surprised that children too feel anxious about changing school. For most the anxieties are short lived and for most the anxiety is tempered by a feeling of excitement about the new school with its new friends and new activities. Changing school is, above all, visible proof that they are growing up.

The same mixed feelings find expression in the views of children throughout the country. Even the same specific horror stories crop up in different areas with only minor variations. The stories about being pushed down the bank, or having one's head pushed down the toilet, recur time and again, however many times the reassuring teacher from the new school denies their authenticity.

There are several easily recognisable groups of fears expressed about changing school. Here are some examples of the fears expressed by a group of fourth year juniors in their final summer term organised in terms of those major themes:

Theme 1: 'Will I get lost?'

> 'On the first day at *** I expect that I will get lost. One of the teachers will tell me where to go and after a month I will get used to ***'
>
> 'I am not looking forward to the first year because it will be very hard to find my way around the school.'

Theme 2: 'Will I get on with my new teachers?'

> 'There's another bit I'm dreading, that is the teacher, I hope she's not strict.'
>
> 'I am worried about going to *** because of maths lessons and the teachers.'

Theme 3: 'Will I get on with the other children?'

> 'The thing I don't like is what the other people are like, because some people from up there say that they will flush your head down the toilet.'
>
> 'I'm not looking forward to the teachers and the older children. I've heard stories about ***, I'll see if they're true.'

Theme 4: 'Will I get on with the new work?'

> 'I think I would rather end my school life at this school because of all the things you have to learn.'
>
> 'Someone told me what they did in science, in science they cut out rats' eyes and cut open their tummies.'

Moving from one stage of schooling to another is what an anthropologist would describe as a 'status passage' and these are often accompanied by 'rites of passage' (Van Gennep, 1960). Measor and Woods (1984) looked at transfer from the perspective of the children and used this approach. They discerned three phases in the process which are presented here much simplified and condensed:

Phase 1 Separation: this takes place during the final term at primary school, is the time of greatest anxiety, of the most myths, and is accompanied by rituals such as visiting the new school and buying the new uniform.

Phase 2 Transition: this covers several stages and lasts most of the first year. Initially the children are mostly hyper-conformist and present a formal front while the teachers try to win them over to the school's official definition of the situation. Later the children make take-over bids and come out with truer identities. This leads to negotiation and the establishment of an acceptable 'modus vivendi'.

Phase 3 Incorporation: after much negotiation the children are incorporated into the social life of the school; this usually happens toward the end of the school year as the school prepares to admit its next intake.

Measor and Woods point out the important part played by myths in the passage from primary to secondary school. They see myths as both expressing and sublimating the children's worries about the impending change of school. They point out that myths are '. . . the key instrument . . . of anticipatory socialisation'. That is, myths help new pupils to know about life in the new school and to adapt to it before they actually join it. Seen from this point of view it is not only impossible to eliminate the retelling of myths but it may well be unwise as well. The House of Commons Select Committee report on achievement in primary schools considered that to rely on such informal information alone would be undesirable:

> Older brothers, sisters and friends are not necessarily the best informants about what the next school will be like. Like some other travellers to strange places they may prefer to emphasise their own superiority with tales of the suffering they bear and the extraordinary sights they have seen. It is as well if the new voyagers can have a glimpse into their future condition.
>
> (House of Commons, 1986, para.11.19)

The recommendation that a 'personal glimpse' should be arranged brings us to a consideration of some of the ways in which heads and teachers can manage the process of transfer in order to minimise disruption and anxiety and promote continuity.

Ways of promoting continuity

The research findings on transfer between schools contain clear guidance on ways of improving current practice. The most fundamental point is that teachers on both sides of the great divide lack up to date and reliable information about the other side. Clearly the first step must be to provide that knowledge.

1. Visits by children to their new school prior to transfer

Almost all children get some form of visit to their new school before they actually transfer. According to the HMI Primary Survey 97 per cent of pupils had such a visit. Some types of visit do more than others to provide information and allay fears. The ORACLE team found that the most effective type of visit was where the children spent a whole day in the school, including dinner and a typical lesson. Least effective was the guided tour where older pupils took newcomers around the school. Galton provides a memorable account of just such a visit:

> I tacked on to one of these parties and was lost three times during the process. We were given snippets of information such as this is where you do mathematics, French etc. Often the door of a classroom would be opened and we would stand in a huddle in the doorway, face the steaming hostility of thirty pairs of eyes in the classroom together with a master who would say, 'Oh! you're coming here next year. I don't expect that I'll be teaching you, but you'll like French, I'm sure.'
>
> (Galton, 1983, p.10)

Some schools arrange longer visits, sometimes with a particular joint project on which the visitors may work with teachers from the new school. In Wiltshire a number of secondary schools have designated primary classrooms which are used by groups from their contributory primary schools at various times throughout the school year. The children use the facilities of the secondary school and some of the secondary school teachers work with the children. Whatever the precise form of the visit, to be effective it needs to provide a realistic taste of what is to come in terms of teaching and of other arrangements like school dinner and playtimes.

2. Visits by teachers to the new school

On nearly every visit made by pupils to their new school they are accompanied by their class teacher, or could be. This should be a valuable opportunity for that teacher to gain more familiarity with the destination school. The teachers' needs will probably be different from those of their pupils and therefore a different programme for the visit will be appropriate. Often the teacher will make a number of visits in succeeding years and could perhaps look at the work in different subjects each year. A little prior planning could ensure that opportunities were provided for the teacher to meet and discuss with teachers from the other school. Some schools go further and arrange the release of teachers to spend time in the other school observing, 'shadowing' pupils, or actually teaching.

3. *Visits by teachers to contributory schools*

These are widely used, by 83 per cent of schools according to the HMI Primary Survey. Normally they consist of a talk about the new school and a chance for the children to ask questions. The prime purpose is to dispel rumours and myths about the maltreatment of newcomers to the new school. They are also often combined with the gathering of information about the children from their current teacher. These visits too have been further developed by some schools. The visiting teacher may take the opportunity to shadow pupils, to observe teaching in progress, to look at pupils' work or to teach alongside the class teacher. The visiting teacher may bring ex-pupils to talk about specific aspects of the new school, or show a video made by pupils about the school.

4. *Transferring information about pupils*

Again this is an almost universal practice, but as HMI in Wales found in their survey of links between primary and secondary schools (Welsh Office, 1986) little direct use was made of cumulative record cards in the design of pupils' learning. An exception to this was the case of pupils with special educational needs. Their records were fuller, often being supplemented with additional information, and more use was made of them by the receiving school. Most primary schools keep samples of children's work as part of their record keeping system, perhaps a selection from each child's folder might be passed to the next school. Information should also be passed on about the schemes of work which the children have been following and the topics they have covered.

5. *Joint meetings of teachers*

Area meetings of headteachers often discuss transfer arrangements. Some also discuss areas of the curriculum, sometimes with an input from a secondary head of department when appropriate. Valuable though these may be there is a need to involve less senior teachers from both schools, since they are the ones who are often in closest contact with the children and who actually do the major part of the teaching.

Some schools arrange joint INSET sessions with their contributory or destination schools.

6. *Involving the parents*

The advent of open enrolment and the increase in parental power will reinforce the already strong trend towards involving parents in the process whereby their children change schools. Most heads have long understood that to involve parents in the process is not only considerate but very cost efficient in terms of time and effort. Changing schools is an anxious time for concerned parents as well as for their child. The main aim of any steps taken to involve parents is to provide information. Reliable information will counteract rumour and myth; let parents know what the new school has to offer their child; reduce parental and child anxiety. The parent governors or the PTA can be an invaluable source of advice and suggestions about how to improve the involvement of parents in the process. They will have been through the experience themselves and now actually know the school. What would they have liked to have known about the school? Whom would they have liked to have met when their child transferred? How could the school have made them and their child more welcome? What wrong impressions did they form of the school at the time of transfer? What have they heard that other schools do and that this one does not? In view of the fact that the parents and their children are, now more than ever, the school's future, the time spent on establishing a relationship of trust, cooperation and accessibility will pay dividends in the future.

Checklist of Things to do to Promote Continuity

A. Pupils' visits

- Have more than one visit
- Arrange typical lessons for pupils to attend
- Show them a range of the work produced in each subject
- Make sure they experience playtimes
- Arrange for pupils to have a school dinner
- Let them use the showers after a P.E. lesson
- Make sure they meet some of the teacher who will actually be teaching them
- Show them a video of a typical school day
- Let ex-pupils from the same school help as hosts

B. Teachers' visits to destination school

- Shadow an ex-pupil for a typical day or half-day
- Have lunch with the children
- Shadow a teacher for a day or half-day
- Discuss what you have seen
- Observe playtime
- Discuss with ex-pupils how they adjusted to the new school
- Discuss ex-pupils with staff of new school
- Look at ex-pupils' work
- Look at a range of children's work
- Discuss teaching approaches with staff
- Feedback and discuss your observations and conclusions with your own colleagues

C. Teachers' visits to contributory schools

- Shadow a pupil for a day or half-day
- Have lunch with the children
- Shadow a teacher for a day or half-day
- Discuss what you have seen
- Observe playtime
- Discuss with prospective pupils their feelings about changing school
- Look at prospective pupils' work
- Look at whole range of children's work
- Discuss teaching approaches with staff
- Arrange to do some teaching
- Discuss your observations and conclusions with your own colleagues

D. Involving parents

- Arrange first meetings at the contributory school, subsequent meetings at destination school
- Invite parents with their children to an Open Day when they can attend 'normal' lessons
- Show parents a video of a typical day
- Display children's work from each department showing progression through the years
- Arrange tours of the school making sure everywhere is clearly signed

- Arrange for mother tongue translations of any information packs
- Arrange for interpreters for non-English speaking parents, and interpreters or signers for deaf parents, if appropriate, and publicise the availability of these facilities
- Make sure parents meet some of the teachers who will actually be teaching their child
- Provide an opportunity for parents to meet their child's tutor in private
- Ask existing parents how the school could improve its performance in this respect
- Remember that these people are the future of the school, any extra trouble taken now will be amply repaid.

It's easy to make a good first impression, much more difficult to change a bad one!

Further reading

Galton, M. and Willcocks, J. (eds.) (1983) *Moving From the Primary Classroom*. London: Routledge and Kegan Paul. The fourth volume of the ORACLE studies, which follows children across the great divide from primary to secondary school.

Derricott, R. (ed.) (1985) *Curriculum Continuity: Primary to Secondary*. Windsor: NFER-Nelson. A collection of papers which together provide an overview of the topic. Several of the chapters give accounts of initiatives which have been designed to improve continuity.

Youngman, M. B. (ed.) (1986) *Mid-Schooling Transfer: Problems and Proposals*. Windsor: NFER-Nelson. An extremely interesting collection of papers which deal with a wide range of issues raised by transfer from school to school. The papers contain many ideas for improving continuity.

CHAPTER 11

Evaluating and Developing the Work of the School

How are we doing? is a question all heads and their staffs ask themselves from time to time. What they are doing is evaluating the work of the school, but they are too often doing it in an unstructured and unsystematic way which does not reveal the full picture of just how effective the school is. Nor does this intuitive approach indicate in a reliable way how that effectiveness might be enhanced. In order to carry out an evaluation which gives a true and accurate picture and which shows how the school can be improved, a structured and systematic approach is essential. This can most readily be achieved using one of the available tools for school self-evaluation (SSE) or whole school review.

Numerous self-evaluation schemes are available and they use a variety of approaches. Experience of SSE shows that merely undertaking a programme of self-evaluation does not necessarily guarantee an improvement in the quality of education in a school. There are, however, some clear messages in these studies of SSE about how to maximise the chances of achieving successful school development.

Interest in SSE grew during the aftermath of Tyndale, Callaghan's Ruskin Speech and the 'Great Debate'. This is not surprising, for the original impetus came from the need to find a cost-effective way of meeting the demands for increased accountability. Even LEAs with the spending power of ILEA did not have sufficient advisers or inspectors to use them as an effective way of providing external evaluation of all their schools. The saga at William Tyndale Junior School proved that point (Auld, 1976). Part of many authorities' response to the growing demands for accountability was to institute schemes of school self-evaluation. Sometimes these schemes were compulsory (e.g. Oxfordshire) while sometimes schools were free to decide whether or not they wished to undertake SSE (e.g. Wiltshire). In most authorities, inspectors or advisers also revived their practice of inspecting schools in order to evaluate their performance. Additionally, in a substantial number of LEAs some form of blanket testing of reading and maths was introduced as another way of checking on schools' performance (e.g. Somerset).

This almost inextricable link with accountability severely restricts the potential for SSE actually to improve the quality of schooling. It is possible to reduce, if not completely eliminate, the accountability element with an evaluation that is initiated by the school rather than the authority. Now that the debate has moved on and few LEAs require schools to use SSE as a way of rendering account, it is easier for heads to use SSE as a purely internally initiated tool for school improvement.

This basic distinction between accountability and development has been commented on by many writers and features in Bolam's (1982) scheme for analysing approaches to SSE. He suggests that each SSE approach can be analysed in terms of its aim, its control and its focus. Aim varies from accountability to development, control may be external or internal, while the focus may be generic (process) or specific (outcome). These distinctions will be useful in considering some of the approaches from which heads and their staffs may choose.

i. The checklist approach

A majority of LEAs have issued guides on school self-evaluation to their schools in the form of booklets of questions covering many aspects of the school's functioning. Not the first, but without doubt the most influential, of these was *Keeping the School Under Review* published in 1977 by the ILEA. This booklet, covering primary and secondary schools, was widely imitated by other LEAs, some simply issuing it to their own schools with a covering letter. The introduction to the booklet makes it clear that it is intended to be a voluntary exercise with a developmental aim. The booklet was replaced in 1982 by a pack containing separate guides for primary, secondary and special schools. The new guides were revised and extended versions of the original. Some samples taken from the section on 'governors, parents and the community' give the flavour of the whole document:

> 1a What contacts are there between the school and the governors?
> b How does the school involve the governors in its life and activities?

11 What are the various kinds of meetings held for parents? What proportion of parents come to each kind? How does the school communicate with those that do not attend?

14 How is the school developing links with the local neighbourhood?
(ILEA, 1982, pp.3–4)

There are certain problems with the checklist approach, however carefully the guide has been constructed. The most obvious and most intractable is that of *prescription*. In spite of the claims in the introductions that they are not intended to be prescriptive, the wording, even the presence, of a particular question gives a clear indication of what the LEA considers to be good practice. A related problem is that of *agenda-setting*. With such schemes the agenda is being set by people outside the school itself. For example, the original ILEA document was written by Staff Inspectors working with a group of heads. Now while this group probably did accurately reflect a senior management view of what schools in general need to evaluate, it is inherently impossible for such an approach to address the unique constellation of circumstances and resulting problems of an individual school. A further problem is that of *validity*. All of the schemes have as one of their prime aims the improvement of the quality of education in schools. Measuring quality is by no means easy and yet the assumption underlying each question is that the response will be indicative of the quality of education which children in that school experience. It is difficult to see how the reliance upon questions of this type may be avoided unless one adopts the much less desirable alternative of relying on 'hard' measures of quality, such as test results. However, it would be preferable if a school staff devised their own questions rather than relied only on those provided by others.

The very process of devising the questions will focus attention on how the staff define 'quality' in their school rather than simply taking it for granted. The Avon self-evaluation scheme made an interesting attempt to avoid this problem by defining 'key questions' which delineated the area of attention and leaving each school to devise 'indicator questions' appropriate to their circumstances:

KEY QUESTION: Are there high standards of behaviour based on mutual respect?

Indicator Questions: Is there an acceptable noise level?
Is the movement of pupils orderly?
Are there any raised voices?
Does a child get a fair hearing?

(Avon County Council, 1980, p.7)

Finally, even though one defines the whole self-evaluation exercise as developmental rather than an act of accountability, that does not actually get rid of the accountability element. In ILEA some governing bodies quite understandably asked their heads whether they were using *Keeping the School Under Review* and, if so, what had come out of it. Indeed the 1982 edition explicitly recognises in its Introduction that it is designed to be helpful in contructing reports to governors.

The lessons of experience in using LEA checklists

Clift *et al.* (1987) contains a number of studies of self-evaluation using LEA checklists. The overall conclusions which they draw from the evidence of SSE in practice are somewhat depressing. However, their rather negative conclusions do contain clear pointers to heads wishing to carry out an effective review of the school. Where SSE was seen as being an exercise in accountability rather than in school development, staff tended to resent the time which it took away from other activities like curriculum development. Those involved did little in the way of collecting data such as children's work, or observing children and teachers at work in the classroom, relying rather on 'individual and collective introspection'. The resulting reports were cautious, superficial, descriptive and showed a marked tendency to identify shortcomings for which the LEA was responsible, such as the lack of a hall or other facilities. Such behaviour is probably sensible when heads and teachers are being held to account but does nothing to improve the quality of the education which the pupils are receiving. To be effective in bringing about school improvement SSE must be voluntary, use a range of data and be firmly focused on development.

ii. An alternative approach: GRIDS

Guidelines for Review and Internal Development in Schools: Primary School Handbook by McMahon *et al.* (1984), known usually by its acronym GRIDS, constitutes a rather different approach to school self-evaluation or school review, which attempts to avoid most of the problems inherent in the checklist approach.

The first step in the GRIDS procedure is for the staff, including the head, to complete a questionnaire covering a wide range of aspects of the life and work of the school. For each item (and there are blank spaces for teachers to add extra items) staff are asked to indicate whether this aspect would benefit from a specific review and also whether they consider that aspect to be an area of strength or weakness. The items are arranged under three headings: curriculum; pupils; staff and organisation. As the final part of this 'initial review', each member of staff is then asked to pick up to three aspects of school life which they consider would benefit from 'specific review' during the next twelve months.

The results of the questionnaire are collated and an area chosen for specific review based upon the expressed priorities of the staff. When the specific review has been carried out using an appropriate range of techniques of data collection, analysis and discussion, some 'action for development' is planned and carried out. The effectiveness of the development work is assessed and then the whole cycle starts again with a fresh aspect of the school's work.

McMahon (1988) herself recognises that this approach may be too formal for some small primary schools and that it is unlikely to appeal to heads who are not already used to involving teachers in the taking of decisions. However the approach has great strengths which make it a very useful tool for the majority of primary schools undertaking a school review.

Strengths of the GRIDS approach to school review

- The agenda is internally set by the teachers themselves. It thus reflects the particular circumstances of the school and the concerns of its staff.
- The whole staff participate. In this way they are more likely to take ownership of the review rather than if evaluation is something which is done to them by others.
- The emphasis is wholly upon development rather than accountability. It is therefore less likely to lead to self-justification and the location of responsibility for weaknesses outside the control of the school itself.
- The taking of action to improve the school is an integral part of the review process. This makes it less likely that the review will fail to actually bring about practical change in the way that the school works.
- School review using GRIDS is inherently a cyclical and continuous process. In this way evaluation is unlikely to be treated as a one-off event.

In her account of using GRIDS, a headteacher (Ebbs, 1987) concluded that the attitudes of the head and of the staff were crucial factors upon which success depended. She found the GRIDS approach to school review a good way of embarking upon review and development work:

> We enjoyed this way of working. We learned a great deal about the curriculum area under review, we chose to continue with this method of working. Most important is that practice has changed . . . . The benefit has been for our children not just teachers or the headteacher.
>
> (Ebbs, 1987, p.183)

Using school review to achieve school improvement

Hopkins, who acted as a consultant of the OECD International School Improvement Project concludes:

> . . . SBR [School Based Review] is an important basis for staff development and one that offers an ongoing and effective means for school improvement.
>
> (Hopkins, 1987, p.168)

He points out that actually doing school review is in itself a means of staff development. Doing it fosters a positive attitude to staff development and can engender an 'innovative orientation amongst a staff and within a school'.

Again in this area of primary school management we find that a crucial factor is the attitude and the resulting behaviour of the head. Clift *et al.* (1987), who are generally somewhat pessimistic about the chances of evaluation achieving actual improvement, put it thus:

> The type of school leader (headteacher or head of department) needed for effective SSE . . . will be one able to defuse professional threat, engender openness and honesty, ensure participation and carry forward reforms.
>
> (Clift *et al*, 1987, p.208)

What needs to be added to that statement is that, given a modicum of those qualities, a programme of school review can be a valuable way for a head to develop a climate in the school which fosters an open, trusting but questioning attitude on the part of the staff that leads to a constant striving for excellence. Having carried out a review, there still remains the vital task of ensuring that the review is used actually to develop the school. One way of doing this is by formulating a school development plan of the type advocated by Norman Thomas.

School development plans

When the ILEA Committee on Primary Education, under the chairmanship of Norman Thomas, reported the results of its inquiry into ways of improving primary schools, it recommended that all primary schools should have a development plan:

> We have seen examples of impressive school development plans in operation . . . . We recommend that every school should have a plan for development, taking account of the policies of the Authority, the needs of the children, the capacities of the staff, and the known views of the parents.
>
> (ILEA, 1985, p.77)

The committee were envisaging a relatively formal arrangement which would apply throughout the ILEA. The plan would be discussed with, and ratified by, the governing body. The authority's inspectorate would be involved in its production, particularly in relation to any resource implications which the development plan might have.

The House of Commons Select Committee on Education, Science and Arts came to a remarkably similar conclusion:

> We recommend that every primary school . . . should be required to operate according to a development plan agreed between it and the governing body and/or LEA . . . The plan should take account of the policies of the Government, LEA, governing body, the capacities of the staff, and the known views of the parents.
>
> (House of Commons, 1986, para 14.167)

There was a link between these two committees. The chairman of one was the adviser to the other. Clearly, the evidence put forward about school development plans was persuasive enough to convince the parliamentarians, subject only to the elimination of 'the needs of the children' in order to make room for 'the policies of the Government'!

What is a school development plan?

The school development plan brings together a number of strands in recent thinking about how to manage schools more effectively. School review, staff appraisal, staff development policies, school-focused INSET, devolved INSET budgets and local financial management all contribute towards the formulation and execution of a school development plan.

The development plan seeks, in a systematic way, to answer these questions about a school:

- Where are we now?
  A process of school review using checklists (e.g. *Keeping the School Under Review*) and GRIDS assesses the school's current effectiveness. Governing body and parental views on performance need to be taken into account at this stage.
- Where are we trying to go?
  Using a cooperative approach which involves the whole staff, a limited number of areas of the school's activities are identified as priorities for development action in order to improve children's learning (again GRIDS can help with this process). Central and local government initiatives, together with governors' policies and parental preferences, should be considered when identifying priorities.
- How do we get there?
  Strategies and plans are formulated for the achievement of the targets identified in the previous stage. The resources needed are identified and earmarked. A time scale is agreed. These may include the purchase of books, equipment and materials as well as appropriate INSET. (Note the connections with the staff development programme.)
- How will we know whether the plan is working?
  The school development plan needs to have built into it specified ways of assessing the impact of action taken under it. This should name those responsible for making that assessment, state how they will do it and when they will do it.

Starting the process

Every stage of the process of formulating a school development plan needs to involve the staff. As the Select Committee put it:

> The plan should be a whole school plan to which all teachers should contribute as class teachers and, to a greater or lesser degree, as coordinators; it should act as a unifying force in the work of staff and children.
>
> (HMSO, 1986, para 13.15)

The school development plan would cover a period of at least one school year but to try and cover more than three years would almost certainly be unrealistic in these times of rapid change. Attached to the plan would be an action sheet which would summarise the action to be taken and by whom, and state what resources will be required. The Thomas Report suggests that the head's report to the governors would consist largely of a report on how implementation of the school development plan was progressing.

In the real world...

Because the use of a school development plan is a matter of choice for a head, rather than of compulsion, there is no need to implement the whole process at once. In fact to try and do so would almost certainly guarantee a reduction in the school's effectiveness in the short term. With rational management procedures of this type it is normally wiser to identify those parts of the procedure which are already being carried out in the school and build from there, selecting additional parts of the procedure as appropriate to the circumstances. Two pieces of advice from Michael Fullan are especially well worth remembering in this context:

> There needs to be a plan and the plan has to acknowledge that it will be departed from.
> The best advice is to start small with expansion in mind.
> (Fullan, 1986, p.82)

The potential of a school development plan for giving some cohesion and unity of purpose to the improvement of the school makes it an attractive proposition which promises to more than repay the initial effort involved.

Further reading

McMahon *et al.* (1984) *Guidelines for Review and Internal Development in Schools: Primary School Handbook*. London: Longmans/Schools Council. This handbook explains the GRIDS approach and contains copyright-free pages for photocopying and distribution within the school. It is essential for any school intending to use GRIDS and useful for any school considering how to approach school review.

Clift, P.S. *et al.* (eds.) (1987) *Studies in School Self-Evaluation*. Lewes: Falmer Press. A varied and interesting collection of papers covering many aspects of school self-evaluation in both the primary and secondary phases. A close reading of some of these papers could help schools to avoid repeating some of the errors of the past.

CHAPTER 12

Staff Selection and Appointment

Talk to any group of teachers about appointment procedures and you will be left in no doubt that much is wrong with the way that most schools select their staff.

Virtually all teachers have their own stock of horror stories about appointments they have been involved in where the outcome was predetermined; where they would not have applied for the job had they known more about it in the first place, or where they were asked inappropriate or irrelevant questions by a group of interviewers who seemed not to know what they were looking for. These stories might be amusing if it were not for the fact that, all too often, they reveal a situation in which staff are appointed on the basis of chance and personal preference rather than on their ability to do the job.

Such evidence is, of course, anecdotal and may be unreliable, exaggerated or out of date, It may be that those who have failed to be appointed to a particular job manage to preserve their self-esteem by portraying the selection process as unfair or irrational. Unfortunately, there is no substantial research relating directly to selection procedures in primary schools. As is often the case in primary school management, one is forced to rely on work carried out in secondary schools or outside of education. When doing this, it is necessary to exercise caution and constantly check the applicability of the research against one's own knowledge and experience and whatever evidence is available.

Current practice

In the case of school staff selection, the principal piece of evidence comes from a research project, the POST project, funded by the DES and carried out by a team from the Open University (Morgan, *et al.*, 1983). They studied the appointment of secondary headteachers in England and Wales between 1980 and 1983. Initially, they examined current procedures for appointment and then, as a piece of action research, developed new procedures which were designed to be both fairer and more efficient. They discovered that current procedures had four main shortcomings:

> (a) selectors had a meagre knowledge of the job and used undeclared criteria;
> (b) the roles of the different groups of selectors were ambiguous;
> (c) the selectors used a restricted selection technology;
> (d) (of most significance) non job-related factors dominated the decision.
>
> (Morgan, 1986, p.153)

Morgan also cites the only other piece of research he could find relating to school staff appointments. This comes from the U.S.A. but is strikingly similar to the POST project in its findings about current procedures. The American team found the same lack of a clear definition of what competencies the selectors were looking for in school principals and the same lack of clarity about how to assess applicants' suitability:

> Every district had a deeply held image of a 'good' principal . . . This image appeared to be widely shared by central administrators, parents and principals themselves. However, time and time again, this fit seemed to rest on personal perceptions of a candidate's physical presence, projections of a certain self confidence, and assertiveness, and embodiment of community values and methods of operation.
>
> (Baltzell and Dentler, 1983)

In a report of a case study carried out on the appointment of a single, temporary primary teacher, Southworth (1987) observed that the head and existing teachers shared a common view of what constituted a 'good teacher'. He sees the holding of such a view as central to the selection process:

> . . . the teachers have certain values concerning what constitues a 'good teacher'. These values are of central importance. Staff selection can be described as a search for someone to fill a vacancy. In order to search for this person you need to know what you are looking for and what a 'good teacher' looks like to you.
>
> (Southworth, 1987, p.112)

This behaviour is not peculiar to school appointments. Salaman and

Thompson studied selection procedures in Ford UK, the BBC and the army. They concluded:

> There is no need for the BBC people to discuss the qualities of the successful candidate (except in terms of such vagueness and confusion that they burst out laughing when one of the panel voices them) because they are entirely confident that they 'know' what BBC producers should be like . . . (p.38)
>
> . . . it was not possible to see the interviews as rigorous and systematic searches for the various qualities upon which organisational suitability and success are supposed to depend . . . (p.56)
>
> (Salaman and Thompson, 1974)

These various findings are not only consistent with one another but also display consistency with the informal primary school staffroom opinions about selection. They raise two major questions. Firstly, does it matter? Secondly, if it does matter, what can be done to improve the current situation?

When appointing staff the primary head, like all of those in the studies above, is trying to appoint the best person for the job. The conclusion of those who have studied various appointment procedures is that the ways in which selectors go about the business of making appointments are unlikely to achieve that end. Given the static nature of the teaching profession and the very substantial and time-consuming difficulties of dealing with an ineffective teacher, time spent on an improved selection procedure which increases the likelihood of appointing good staff is time well spent. The present system depends too heavily on intuition and, accordingly, leaves too much to chance.

Designing an effective staff selection procedure

The basic aim when appointing staff is, of course, to find the best available person for the job, so, logically, there are three steps in any process designed to achieve that aim:

- Define the job to be filled.
- Identify the skills, knowledge, attitudes and values necessary to do that job.
- Decide upon what will count as evidence of the possession of those competencies and attributes.

Each of these steps translates into activities which, when taken together, will comprise what Morgan (1988) calls a 'rational selection procedure' in contrast to what is all too often at present a capricious and irrational process.

1. Defining the job – preparing a job description

The vacancy will have arisen either because of the departure of a teacher or because the staffing establishment is being increased. In either case the starting point should be the same: what does the school need? There is a danger that when someone leaves the selection procedure starts with an assumption that a replacement for the person is what is needed. This may in fact be what the school needs, but the opportunity to make an appointment tends to arise infrequently and should be seized as a chance to influence the development of the school in a potentially decisive way. The more senior the post, the more potential there is for this sort of development.

The construction of a job description is a task best undertaken co-operatively with the staff. There are two main reasons for this. Firstly, the obvious one that two minds are better than one. That is, the job description is likely to be better technically, in terms of its comprehensiveness, appropriateness and realism. Secondly, if the head is trying to promote a more collegial approach to the management of the school then this is an opportunity to foster participation and cohesiveness amongst the staff. It can be part of the process of building a consensus on such issues as where the school is going and what the school stands for. Furthermore, in a collegial school the staff work as a team and, as Southworth (1987) points outs, the new teacher will be expected to function as part of that team. It would therefore be strange, to say the least, not to involve that team in the selection of its new member. Indeed, these arguments in favour of staff participation also apply at later stages of the selection process.

There are many ways of handling the practicalities of participation in the preparation of a job description. It may be done as a group task, brainstorming on a blank flip-chart sheet and then discussing the result. Or the staff that the new teacher will work with most closely might be invited to prepare the first draft, which could then be discussed with the whole staff. Or the head might choose to prepare the first draft, circulate copies to the teachers, and then discuss it at a staff meeting. Or the school might already have a set of regularly up-dated job descriptions for existing staff, which could be used as part of the discussion process. Most LEAs have generic job descriptions which similarly could be used in that way. The choice of method might depend on how well established participation is in the school. A staff who are used to working cooperatively, and who already share a common set of values about the school and its developments, would gain from the less structured brainstorming approach while a less confident staff might need the head to set the agenda more closely by preparing a first draft for them.

If the school is one which constantly reviews and evaluates its progress in a structured way then the review process is likely to have pointed up the school's needs. It may be that the head has taken the advice of the Thomas Report (ILEA, 1985) and the school already has a school development plan (see Chapter 11), in which case this too will be useful in assessing what the school needs from the new appointment.

The job description should contain the following elements:

- Job title
- Job tasks, duties and responsibilities (divided into areas or categories; e.g. teaching, administrative, curriculum, pastoral)
- Role relationships (to whom and for whom one is responsible; with whom one works, within and outside the school)

There is a need to keep a balance, when constructing a job description, between being sufficiently specific, so that the selectors know what post they are trying to fill, and yet keeping enough flexibility to allow unexpected special interests to be utilised to the school's advantage. Job descriptions should not be set in concrete but rather should be regularly reviewed and amended in the light of the school's changing needs and of the individual teacher's professional development. This can best be done as part of the school's ongoing staff development programme which may include an appraisal interview (see Chapter 13).

2. Defining the competencies – preparing a person profile

Having produced the job description, the next step is to analyse the skills, knowledge, attitudes and values which are needed in order to do that job effectively in the particular context of the school. Everard and Morris (1985), from whom I have taken the term 'personal profile', suggest dividing the desired competencies into 'essential' and 'desirable'. This seems like a sensible suggestion which avoids the much more time-consuming alternative of constructing a prioritised list while still directing the selectors' attention to the fact that some of the competencies are more important than others.

In the traditional intuitive selection process this is where the process often starts. The person specification or profile, though, is derived from the unexamined images which the selectors have formed in their minds of what constitutes a 'good teacher'. These images may or may not be shared and may or may not fortuitously coincide with what the school actually needs. It is an interesting question, but not particularly relevant here, to ask how these images are constructed. For lay selectors the answer seems to be that they are an amalgam of images presented in fiction, film and television, and memories of teachers they knew when they were pupils themselves. Clearly, this has little place in a rational selection procedure. The person profile should rather be based upon a clear analysis of the school's needs as a dynamic and changing organisation.

One could produce a generic person profile for the post of (say) a Main Professional Grade Junior teacher, and that might have some limited use as one of the inputs to the process of constructing a person profile for a particular vacancy, but the best starting point would be the jointly prepared job description produced as step one. As in step one, the arguments for also approaching this task in a collegial way are compelling.

3. *Determining and assessing the evidence*

Having completed the job description and person profile, the focus then shifts to deciding what evidence the selectors are going to seek in order to assess an applicant's suitability for the vacancy.

The fundamental problem that selectors face here is similar to that faced by the punter looking for which horse to back in the 2.30 at Goodwood. It is a problem of prediction. Like the race-goer, one can study form. In the case of teachers, this means assessing past performance as a teacher and using that as a guide to likely future performance.

There are problems with that approach. The situation which the new appointee is entering may be unlike the one they are leaving or the new post may have greater or different responsibilities than the old one. This is especially likely to be the case if the new post involves promotion, say, to Deputy Head, when the applicants will have had little opportunity to display the competencies identified in the person profile.

Another approach which is being used increasingly for appointments in commerce and industry is to try and assess the candidates' latent abilities. This typically involves putting them in situations which resemble the new job in some way and observing their behaviour, or giving them psychometric tests which purport to measure aspects of their personality which are held to be important for the effective execution of the new role. The assessment of demonstrated or latent abilities is best regarded as a complementary rather than an alternative approach. Current practice tends to rely almost exclusively on the assessment of demonstrated ability while any judgement about latent ability is based solely upon hunch. Even the assessment of past performance is frequently carried out in an inefficient and unsystematic way.

The assessment of past performance

Traditionally, this has been done by means of the application form or letter, references and an interview. Studies of appointment procedures, some of which I referred to earlier, contain in their criticisms clear indications of how the effectiveness of such techniques may be improved. The POST project (Morgan *et al.*, 1983) is especially helpful here, particularly their later handbook (Morgan *et al.*, 1984) relating to the appointment of secondary heads, which contains ideas which may be adapted to other appointments. The POST team also draw attention to the need to consider carefully how the resulting evidence is to be evaluated by the selectors.

1. The application form

LEA application forms differ considerably in the range of questions which they ask and some include a space for a letter of application while others indicate that a letter may accompany the form. There is a core of information, mostly relating to qualifications and previous employment, which is common to all. The POST team designed a new form which organised the information so that is was more easily retrievable but the biggest change was the substitution of structured questions for the open letter of application:

> Describe in some detail how you see your previous professional career as relevant to your application for headship now. Include in your description your perceptions of the usefulness to you of any in-service courses you have attended in your preparations for headship.
>
> (Morgan *et al.*, 1983, p.117)

While that question applies specifically to headship it would be an easy matter to adapt it to, say, a primary deputy headship. The basic principle of this approach is to ensure that every applicant actually addresses the same issues so that the quality of their responses may be compared in a way that is less easy in an open letter. The questions would be generated by the specific job description and person profile but other examples, some adapted from POST, might be:

- What in your view are the essential aims of primary education in the context of this school?
- Describe in detail an example of how and why you enabled children for whom you were responsible to learn from first hand real experience.
- Explain how you have fostered closer links between school and home in your present post.
- How do you cater in your teaching for children's individual needs?

In framing such questions it is important to relate them closely to the job description and person profile. When this type of application form was used in the POST project, the number of forms returned completed was significantly reduced. This might have been due to the demanding nature of the form or to the fact that the form was sent out with the job description and full details of the school. It does suggest, however, that the extra time that it takes to prepare this type of form has its reward in a reduction in the number of less serious applicants.

2. *References*

POST found that the main problems associated with references were their blandness, their lack of connection with the competencies that were relevant to the job, their use of 'code', and their reliance upon anecdotal rather than systematic evaluative evidence. They may, of course, also be out of date, inaccurate, biased or intentionally misleading. Clearly not all of these possible problems can be completely avoided, however well structured the selection might be. POST tried to reduce them by using a tightly constructed, pre-coded reference form which focused directly upon the demands of the job; but this was, in a number of cases, unpopular with the referees. A more acceptable alternative would be the use of specific headings or topics upon which the referee is asked to comment:

- Has the applicant demonstrated an ability to extend his/her influence beyond his/her own classroom? Please give examples if appropriate.
- In what ways has the applicant contributed to the extra-curricular life of the school?

- What is your assessment of the candidate's matching of work to the needs of the children in his/her class?

Again the questions should derive from the specific job description and person profile and the referee should receive copies of these in addition to full details of the school.

The assessment of future potential

1. The interview

It is not only in school appointments that interviews are used for staff selection. In spite of a growing body of evidence which shows the interview to be unreliable as a predictor of future performance, it continues to be used in most fields of employment. Because it is so widely used, it has been widely studied, and the findings of these studies are remarkably consistent. Some of the findings contain clear indications of how interviewing practice could be improved though, taken as a whole, they would support the view that interviews are inherently unreliable and should therefore be allowed to play only a minor role in any selection procedure.

- Interviewers reach their decision about each candidate very early in the interview, under four minutes in one study (Webster, 1964)
- Physically attractive candidates are more likely to be appointed (Gilmore *et al.*, 1986)
- Interviewers are poor at recalling information about the candidates (Carlson, 1971)
- Most interviewers do not take notes (Morgan *et al.*, 1983)
- An average candidate who follows several poor candidates is seen as particularly good (Carlson, 1971)
- In headship interviews more personal questions are asked than any other category (Morgan *et al.*, 1983)
- In taking a final decision in headship interviews selectors give more weight to personality and personal qualities than to job related criteria (Morgan *et al.*, 1983)
- Even in highly structured selection procedures the interviews is used to justify and explain the decision rather than to guide it (Salaman and Thompson, 1974)

Interviewing practice can be improved by following certain procedures:

(1) The interviewers need to be fully aware of the job description and the person profile. They need to discuss, and to agree upon the questions which will elicit information that is related to the job.
(2) Interviewers should keep notes upon each candidate using a record sheet which relates to the person profile.
(3) Each member of the interviewing panel should be identified by a clear sign which also shows their role.
(4) Invite each candidate to bring a portfolio of work from children they have taught which they may use to illustrate how they work as a teacher.
(5) All of the information relevant to each candidate should be available to each selector at the point of decision. This information needs to be compiled in a systematic way so that each source of information may be given proper consideration

Further suggestions for improving interview practice may be found in Morgan *et al.*, (1984).

2. *Analogous tests*

In view of the shortcomings of each of the components of the selection process which we have considered so far, it is hardly surprising that there should be a rising level of interest in some other technique for assessing candidates' performance in a new job. Analogous tests try to simulate an aspect of the job and then assess the candidate's reaction. This is believed to give a better indication of how they might perform the new role. Obviously there are possible difficulties associated with this method too. The tests may not reflect the job tasks in a fair and representative way, and the artificiality of the test situation may produce a response which is not typical of how the candidate would behave in real life. However, as a way of supplementing the other information about each candidate, all of which is subject to its own limitations, these tests seem able to give an additional perspective on the candidate's likely future performance.

Analogous tests should of course be generated from the specific job description and person profile but the examples given might act as stimuli for the imagination.

It might be thought that tests of this sort are unnecessarily gruelling for the candidates. Some LEAs have started using exercises of this sort as part of the selection procedure for primary heads. My experience of applicants who have been subjected to this type of test suggests that, while the tests were seen as more demanding, most applicants felt that

Examples of Analogous Tests

- ☐ An angry parent is waiting for you as you approach your classroom at 8.30 a.m. She tells you that her ten-year-old child has been awake all night worrying about the residential trip to Swanage which you have planned. She does not now want her daughter to go. What do you do?
- ☐ Three children who are normally the best of friends have been quarrelling in the playground at lunchtime. They refuse to continue working together on the problem-solving exercise which is still uncompleted. How will you handle this?
- ☐ You are the deputy head of an infant school and you have arrived at school to find that the head has had a serious accident on the way to school. A letter marked 'urgent' is on the head's desk. It is from a neighbour who complains about the behaviour of the children on the way home from school. Write a letter of reply and say what other action you would take.
- ☐ A reading test shows that half of your new class of eight-year-olds are more than one year behind the average for their age. What do you do about this?
- ☐ You are responsible for the Infant Department and the head tells you that a physically handicapped six-year-old child is to join the school next week. Explain how you would (a) prepare for the child's admission, and (b) ensure that the child's needs continued to be met.

they did at least have a fairer opportunity to show their level of competence than in the normal interview situation alone.

In the USA, principals felt so strongly that normal selection procedures were deficient in terms of assessing their job-related competence that they set up an assessment centre through their union, the National Association of Secondary School Principals (NASSP). Here, trained assessors use a battery of situational and analogous tests to produce an assessment report. The use of assessment centres is also to be found in the UK in fields outside education. For example, the army have for some years been using a combination of analogous tests, personality tests, references and interviews to select candidates for officer training. Some independent business consultants provide a similar service to commerical clients.

Although I have been arguing for a much more structured and systematic approach to staff selection, which uses a range of information sources that are closely linked to the competencies actually required for the job, I do not wish to suggest that this would completely eliminate all of the uncertainties from making new appointments. Any predictive process is inherently uncertain. Rather, one is seeking to reduce the uncertainties by attending to the known defects of the present procedures.

Salaman and Thompson (1974) researched a range of selection procedures including the highly systematised army Regular Commissions Board and concluded:

> In the actual event the more or less formalised schemes were used not to guide and determine the interview, but to justify and explain . . . how the interview decision was reached.
>
> (Salaman and Thompson, 1974, p.51)

Even a highly systematic procedure then does not necessarily alter the fundamental nature of the selection process. The selectors are still looking for someone who will share their set of values and their view of the world. Furthermore, the systematic procedure can simply provide the rational grounds to legitimate that choice.

Coulson (1987) argues that headteachers need to be able to follow hunches, on the grounds that the fragmented nature of their jobs leads to intuitive and spontaneous responses rather than planned and analytical responses. Indeed he states that:

> There can be little doubt, however, that outstanding heads are the ones who can couple effective right-hemisphere processes (hunch, judgement, synthesis and so on) with effective processes of the left (articulateness, logic, analysis and so on).
>
> (Coulson, 1987, p.24)

However, it is not a mechanistic system which I am advocating but rather one which, unlike current practice, does not rely on hunch alone but which treats candidates equitably and gives proper weight to their demonstrated and likely future ability.

Further reading

Morgan, C. *et al.* (1983) *The Selection of Secondary School Headteachers*. Milton Keynes: Open University Press. Although this report of the POST project is specifically concerned with the selection of secondary heads, the arbitrary, amateur and intuitive system it reveals is not unique to that phase of schooling nor to that level of appointments. There is much here of relevance to anyone who is involved in appointing staff at any level in a primary school.

Morgan, C. *et al.* (1984) *A Handbook on Selecting Senior Staff for Schools*. Milton Keynes: Open University Press. This is the sequel to the POST report. It incorporates checklists for the organiser to use in the appointment of secondary heads but it could be adapted for other appointments in primary schools. There is an interesting collection of in-basket materials and a guide to constructing such materials.

CHAPTER 13

Staff Development

The staff are the most important resource in the school. Their development should therefore be one of the prime concerns of the headteacher who is seeking excellence in the education that the children in the school receive. Yet few schools have a coherent staff development policy which systematically seeks to assess and meet the needs of the school and of the teachers. Most schools have what Lyons (1976) called a 'peripheral' approach which:

> . . . is characterised by ad hoc provision for individuals or to meet particular circumstances. Hand-to-mouth attendance at courses, conferences and seminars (however good these might be) often passed under the guise of . . . staff development.
>
> (Lyons, 1976, p.138)

This individual-needs or job-needs orientated approach contrasts with the 'integral' approach with its coherent policies which first identify, and then seek to meet, the needs of the individual teacher and of the school.

Staff development then involves much more than simply drawing teachers' attention to the existence of courses being offered by the LEA or the local college or university and encouraging them to attend. In-service training (INSET) is an important part of a staff development programme but is no more than one element in the programme.

It is necessary first to identify the needs of the school and the teachers. Having identified those needs, there are then various ways of meeting them. INSET may be the appropriate way in some cases but there are many other possibilities which ought to be considered.

Recent developments

1. Policy initiatives

Several recent policy initiatives at local and national levels have combined to emphasise the desirability of every school having a carefully designed staff development policy. All schools have five 'Baker Days' which may form a valuable part of the school's staff development programme if their use is carefully planned and executed within the framework provided by a staff development policy. LEAs are required to demonstrate that their bids for Grant Related Inservice Training (GRIST) funds are based upon the needs of the schools. An 'integral approach' to staff development enables heads to respond more convincingly and more effectively to the consultation procedures initiated by the LEA. Many LEAs also devolve a proportion of the INSET budget, in an earmarked grant, directly to the schools. Control of at least a part of this budget gives heads an opportunity to take decisions which ensure that the staff development programme is actually executed.

2. School effectiveness studies

Recent research on school effectiveness also supports the desirability of a planned approach to staff development. The ILEA *Junior School Project* investigated INSET rather than staff development *in toto* and found that there was a subtle connection between school effectiveness and INSET attendance. A general encouragement to attend courses as often as teachers wished was associated with poorer pupil progress. However, where the encouragement to attend courses was more specific and for a particular reason, course attendance was associated with better pupil progress. The research team concluded:

> These results do not imply that teachers should not attend courses (the proportion of staff who had been on courses was related positively to writing progress, attendance, and attitudes to school and to mathematics), but rather that **a school-based policy was beneficial.**
>
> (Mortimore *et al.*, 1988, p.224 [my emphasis])

Planning a Staff Development Policy

What then is the planning process by which a school can devise an effective staff development policy? McMahon and Turner (1988) produced a useful description of the stages involved in planning and implementing a school or LEA staff development programme which I have modified slightly. I intend to use this to examine the issues which heads will need to consider in constructing a staff development policy, while the next section will look at what such a policy might contain.

A Staff Development Policy Planning Cycle

(1) Assess the role of staff development within the overall school development plan.
(2) Identify individual and school needs.
(3) Establish priorities in the light of 1.
(4) Plan a programme of activities to meet prioritised needs.
(5) Implement the programme.
(6) Monitor and evaluate the programme.
(7) Review the policy and restart cycle.

Adapted from: McMahon and Turner (1988)

1. Assessing the role of staff development within the overall school development plan

Staff development is an integral part of developing the school, not something which may be thought of as an optional extra and which relates only to the needs and interests of the individual teacher. Effective schools have a strong, purposeful ethos which stresses high standards of achievement and behaviour. The staff development policy should be planned in such a way that it helps cultivate and sustain such an atmosphere in the school.

2. Identifying individual and school needs

The identification of needs is a crucial if difficult step. Traditionally INSET has concentrated upon the individual needs of the teachers as they themselves identified them. Currently there is an emphasis on INSET which is focused upon the school. A balance needs to be kept between the interests of individual teachers and those of the school where they currently work. Any procedure for the identification of needs must enable both types of need to be recognised. The identification of school needs is best accomplished by a programme of school review. School review and self-evaluation are discussed in detail in Chapter 11. Individual teachers' needs are best identified by a form of appraisal which focuses firmly on professional development rather than on managerial control.

Appraisal as a means of needs identification

Appraisal is viewed with mistrust by many teachers, who see it as an attack on their professional autonomy, as another example of managerial control contributing to their 'deskilling'. This view is not surprising because appraisal – a management technique derived from industry – is often used in just such a way in industry, and at various stages has been proposed for schools as a way of 'weeding out weak teachers' or of identifying able teachers who should receive 'merit pay'. The DES sponsored pilot schemes of teacher appraisal have largely eschewed the use of appraisal as a technique for controlling the teaching force. Cumbria, for example, which uses a whole school review to set the climate and context for individual appraisal, claims that its scheme has resulted in the '. . . removal of negative feelings towards appraisal' (NDC, 1988, p. 13). However, Suffolk, which has a longer track record in teacher appraisal than most authorities, is rather more cautious on this topic in its interim report:

> . . . apprehension – despite constant reassurance there is disbelief that the intentions of 'them' (government, LEAs) are honourable.
>
> (NDC, 1988, p.38)

It seems that individual heads are quite capable of implementing appraisal schemes which are intended to foster professional development and which are indeed perceived in that way by their staff. The prerequisite for doing this is an established atmosphere within the school of trust, openness and professional cooperation. It seems likely that a national scheme would encounter considerable mistrust in those schools where the atmosphere is less conducive to professional development.

Most people think of appraisal as synonymous with appraisal interviewing, but the interview is just one, albeit important, element of an appraisal scheme. The elements to be found in the six pilot schemes are:

- initial review discussion
- self evaluation by the teacher
- classroom observation of the teacher
- appraisal interview.

There are other elements which could be included. For example, an appraisal scheme might also make use of colleagues' views of the teacher's performance and written documents like pupils' work, test results, and work forecasts and records.

The aim of any appraisal scheme intended to foster professional development would be to develop the teacher's performance and thus enhance the pupils' learning rather than simply to form judgements about the teacher's performance. That is to say, it would be formative rather than summative. An appraisal carried out with just such a developmental intention and which used a range of techniques would generate reliable information about the teachers' needs, both as individuals and as part of a team. This, together with the information derived from the school review, would provide the data upon which decisions could then be taken about relative priorities in the school's staff development policy.

Heads have needs too! – management development

It is easy to overlook the fact that the head, too, has professional development needs. In the case of the head, as with other senior staff, these would be both management development needs as well as teacher development needs.

Management development is a concept which has been popularised in the educational world largely by the efforts of the National Development Centre for School Management Training (NDC) at Bristol University. It refers to the process of improving the management of schools in order to increase the school's effectiveness. Management development is therefore a part of staff development, and any staff development policy should include a management development policy covering any member of staff with managerial responsibilities. This would be based upon an assessment of the needs of the school and of the members of staff who have a management responsibility. In its useful handbook for primary schools on management development, the NDC points out that these individual needs are likely to be affected by a number of factors:

- their age
- their race and gender
- their job stage, i.e.
  - the preparatory stage (e.g. when they are preparing to apply for a new job)
  - the appointment stage (when they are selected or rejected)
  - the induction stage (e.g. first two years in post)
  - the in-service stage which includes development and regeneration (e.g. 3–5, 6–10, 11 + years in post)
  - the transitional stage (e.g. promotion, redeployment, retirement)

(McMahon and Bolam, 1988, p.6)

When the needs have been identified, a programme of activities is then drawn up and implemented to meet those needs. In this way the management needs of the school and the staff would not be overlooked but would be included in the staff development programme.

A pool of wasted talent?

If one studies the statistics published each year by the DES it quickly becomes apparent that, within the teaching workforce, there is a group of teachers who seem to be neglected and overlooked when it comes to professional development and career advancement. The extraordinary feature of this group is that they are not members of some exploited minority group. On the contrary, they are the majority of the teaching staff within every category of primary school. Teachers who belong to this group have a much lower chance of receiving an incentive allowance and their chances of achieving headship are very much lower. So, who are these teachers whose talent is not being used to its maximum? They are women.

According to the DES figures (DES, 1986) 74.5 per cent of all teachers in 5–11 primary schools are women yet only 29.7 per cent of heads of such schools are women. In the case of junior schools, 65.7 per cent of the teachers are women while only 18.9 per cent of the heads are women. In all forms of primary school, including nursery schools, we find that 77.6 per cent of all primary teachers are women whereas only 44.9 per cent of primary heads are women. These figures are of course reflecting, and substantiating, what anyone who has ever attended a meeting of primary heads has long known to be the case. Women are seriously under-represented in senior posts in primary schools. Nor is there anything unusual about the UK. In fact, our figures are rather better than those for most western industrial countries: Australia, USA, New Zealand, Canada and Finland, for example, all have worse under-representation problems (Schmuck, 1986).

There has been a long, and still continuing, debate about the reasons why there are too few women heads. The career break to raise childen is an obvious career hurdle for many women. Some see women as having been socialised into accepting male dominance at work as elsewhere in their lives, resulting in few women coming forward as applicants for headship. Others point to the fact that men are already established in the senior positions and tend to favour other men when sponsoring candidates for promotion.

The role of a sponsor does seem to be important in developing a career in teaching, as elsewhere. Many heads can identify an individual, usually a head, sometimes an adviser, who first prompted them to think of themselves as 'headship material'. Heads tend to 'talent spot' teachers whom they regard as worthy of promotion. A teacher who is so identified will then be 'groomed' for promotion by being given responsibilities within the school, encouraged to attend courses, invited to join working parties and to help with INSET. Indeed, some heads pride themselves on the number of heads they have 'grown' in their school. The problem here is that heads, most of whom are men, tend to spot that talent more frequently in other men than in women.

The factors in our society which act to limit women's career development are scarcely susceptible of change by a primary headteacher managing a school. However, the individual primary head *can* do something about the way in which he sponsors teachers for promotion. What is needed first is a consciousness of the problem. One needs to be aware that the best people are probably not getting to the top of the career ladder. We are choosing our heads from much too small a group within the profession. Secondly, one needs to become conscious of the tendency to see promotion potential in men rather than women and act to ensure that women are properly represented amongst the teachers being groomed for promotion. A systematic staff development programme based on a thorough needs assessment could and should do much to make proper use of what is without doubt a pool of under-used talent.

3. Establishing priorities in the light of the school development plan

Resources are never likely to be sufficient to meet all of the identified needs. This means that hard decisions will have to be made about which needs should take precedence. The priorities will reflect the particular circumstances of the school so it is difficult to generalise about this issue. There are, however some general principles which should guide the choice.

Firstly, whenever a decision is going to result in some people being disappointed it is better to involve the whole group in the decision making process. Participation will not avoid disappointment but it will at least lead to the disappointed understanding how the decision was taken and realising that the grounds for the decision were rational rather than arbitrary. Participation will also help build or maintain consensus within the staff. Furthermore, staff development is not something which is done to people; to be effective it must be something to which they feel committed. A share in the decision making will increase the teachers' sense of ownership of the staff development programme.

Secondly, the priorities should flow directly from the agreed development plan for the school. In this way, the staff development programme will be seen as an integral part of the development of the school rather than as a set of arbitrary favours bestowed by the head.

Thirdly, a balance must be kept between the needs of the individual teacher and those of the school. One of the dangers of a school-focused staff development programme is that it can too easily ignore the need for individual professional development. It would be difficult to justify the release of a teacher to take a masters degree in management solely in terms of the immediate pay-off to the school. Yet advanced study of this sort may well be vital to the teacher's longer term career aim of joining an LEA advisory service or of becoming an HMI. If opportunities for personal professional development are constantly withheld in favour of those with a quick pay-off for the school, the result will be a staff of frustrated extended professionals or contented restricted professionals. Either of which alternatives will reduce the school's effectiveness in the longer term.

Finally, and this is connected with the point about balancing the needs of the organisation and those of the individual, the appraisal scheme will quickly become discredited if the needs which it identifies are persistently ignored in the staff development programme.

4. Planning the programme of activities to meet the needs

At this stage in the process it is important to remember that staff development is not just a new term for INSET. The terms are not conterminous. INSET is just one of the possible ways of meeting a staff development need.

The list of possible staff development activities is not exhaustive – many more ideas may be found in Oldroyd *et al.* (1984). The list contains a mixture of activities which require external support and those that do not; a mixture of activities which require extra resourcing and those that do not; and a mixture of activities which focus on the needs of the school and those which focus more on the needs of the individual teacher. Again, it is important to keep a balance between the different types of activity, for another danger in the present

Possible Staff Development Activities

- ☐ Visits to other schools or institutions
- ☐ Observing another teacher at work
- ☐ Teacher exchange
- ☐ Working alongside another teacher
- ☐ Twinning with a class in another school
- ☐ Working with an advisory teacher or adviser
- ☐ Visit from an adviser
- ☐ Working with students in training
- ☐ Working with lecturer from teacher training institution
- ☐ Using a consultant to facilitate team building
- ☐ Being observed by a colleague
- ☐ Being part of a working party
- ☐ Leading a staff discussion
- ☐ Providing INSET for others
- ☐ Working in a cluster of small schools
- ☐ Teaching a different age group
- ☐ Carrying out a small-scale piece of action research
- ☐ Taking on new responsibilities
- ☐ Changing one's responsibilities
- ☐ Taking an OU course in one's own time
- ☐ School review
- ☐ Running educational evenings for parents
- ☐ Liaising with feeder schools or playgroups
- ☐ Liaising with destination schools
- ☐ School-based workshop 'Baker Days'
- ☐ Attending a course
- ☐ Studying for an Advanced Diploma or Master's degree

emphasis on school-focused staff development is that the school can become too inward-looking and insular. One benefit which heads and teachers often remark upon when attending university-based programmes is the opportunity to exchange ideas with teachers working in other authorities. However lively a school might be, it still has no monopoly upon good ideas and would soon become a backwater if its staff remained cut off from stimuli from outside.

Effective INSET

In recent years some interesting findings have emerged about just what constitutes effective INSET. These are discussed in Chapter 9 but at this point it is worth reminding ourselves that mere attendance at a course, however well run, is unlikely to produce actual change in the classroom. To be effective, a programme of staff development must include all these elements identified by Joyce and Showers (1980):

- Presentation
- Demonstration
- Practice
- Feedback
- Coaching

If including all of these elements means that the scope of the staff development programme has to be less extensive, then that will be fully justified by the gain in effectiveness.

5. Implementing the programme

Provided the planning stage has been thoroughly carried out, this is relatively uncomplicated. In some areas competent and reliable supply teachers are hard to find and thought needs to be given to how any cover is to be provided for classes whose teacher is absent during school time because of a staff development activity. In larger schools, heads can often use these opportunities to maintain and develop their own teaching skills by taking the class themselves.

6. Monitoring and evaluating the programme

The basic question to be addressed here is whether the programme is actually meeting the needs in the way that was intended. The staff development policy should state both *who* is responsible for evaluating the programme and *how* it will be done.

7. Reviewing the policy and restarting the cycle

The final step emphasises that staff development is a continuous process rather than an event. The school has developing needs as it changes, and as the environment in which it works changes. The teachers too have changing needs as they progress through their working lives. The staff development policy must recognise this dynamic.

Getting started

At this point constructing a staff development policy may be looking a little daunting. However, most schools will not be starting from a blank sheet; they will already have in operation the basics of a programme, even though it may well be unsystematic and uncoordinated. As in most things, the best plan is to start with what you have got. A full staff development policy using the process outlined above may well take time to develop but an incremental approach, building gradually towards that objective, could be instituted fairly rapidly. As Michael Fullan pithily put it:

> The best advice is to start small with expansion in mind.
>
> (Fullan, 1986, p.82)

Constructing a staff development policy

What then are the elements of a staff development policy? What should it include? What might it look like? Hewton (1988) reports the results of his work with a group of schools in East Sussex preparing and implementing staff development policies. His book indicates some of the possible answers to these questions. From his analysis of draft policies he found that certain elements recurred and this list, while not definitive, provides a useful framework which could be used by a school devising its first school development policy.

The Elements of a Staff Development Policy

1. *Aims and rationale*
2. *Structure:* defines who does what in respect of identifying needs, planning, implementing and evaluating the programme.
3. *Programme of activities:* sets out details, with costs, of who will undertake which staff development activities and when.
4. *Evaluation:* defines who will undertake evaluation of the programme and how they will do it.

Adapted from: Hewton (1988) Chapter 7

Many of the developments in primary school management practice are complementary. School review or self-evaluation, school development plans, appraisal and staff development policies are intertwined in a mutually supporting way and all move in the same direction of a 'thinking' school which is constantly seeking to improve the quality of the education which its pupils experience.

Further reading

Easen, P. (1985) *Making School-centred INSET Work*. Beckenham: Open University Press/Croom Helm. This book is part of an OU course by the same name but is capable of being used on its own independently of the course. It contains a wealth of ideas and practical suggestions for anyone wishing to make better use of 'Baker Days'. It is particularly useful for heads wishing to develop the interpersonal relationships amongst the staff.

Hewton, E. (1988) *School-Focused Staff Development*. Lewes: Falmer Press. This is a readable account of a project which the author undertook with a group of schools in East Sussex in which they formulated and operated staff development policies. The book would be extremely helpful to a head who is keen to use this approach to staff development.

References

Abbott, D. (1986) *Teachers' Reactions to the Publication of HM Inspectors' Reports on Schools*. Unpublished Diploma dissertation: University of Bristol.

Acker, S. (1988) *Managing the Drama: The Headteacher's Work in an Urban Primary School*. Unpublished paper: University of Bristol.

Arnold, M. (1867) 'General Report for the Year', in Maclure, J. S. (ed) (1965) *Educational Documents England and Wales 1816 to the present day*. London: Methuen.

Atherton, G (1982) *The book of the school: a study of Scottish school handbooks issued to pupils and their parents*. Glasgow: Scottish Consumers Council.

Auld, R. (1976) *Report of the Public Inquiry into William Tyndale Junior and Infant Schools*. London: ILEA.

Avon County Council (1980) *Report of the Working Party on In-School Evaluation*. Bristol: Avon County Council.

Ball, S. J. (1987) *The Micro-Politics of the School*. London: Methuen.

Baltzell, C. & Dentler, R. (1983) *Selecting American School Principals. A Research Report*. Cambridge, Mass.: Abt Associates.

Barker Lunn, J. C. (1982) 'Junior Schools and their Organisational Policies'. *Educational Research*, **24**: 250–261.

Barker Lunn, J. C. (1984) 'Junior School Teachers: their methods and practices'. *Educational Research*, **26**: 178–188.

Baron, G. (1974) 'Some Aspects of the "Headmaster Tradition" ' in Houghton, V. *et al.* (eds) (1975) *Management in Education*. London: Ward Lock.

Bastiani, J. (1978) *Written communication between home and school: a report*. Nottingham: University of Nottingham.

Bealing, D. (1972) 'The organisation of Junior School Classrooms'. *Educational Research*, **14**: 231–235.

Belasco, J. A. & Alutto, J. A. (1972) 'A Typology for participation in Organizational Decision Making'. *Administrative Science Quarterly* **17**.

Bennis, W. G., Benne, K. D. & Chin, R. (1969) *The Planning of Change*. New York: Holt, Rinehart & Winston.

Blau, P. M. (1964) *Exchange and Power in Social Life*. New York: John Wiley.

Board of Education (1926) *Report of the Consultative Committee on The Education of the Adolescent*. (The Hadow Report). London: HMSO.

Board of Education (1931) *Report of the Consultative Committee on the Primary School* (The Hadow Report). London: HMSO.

Bolam, R. (1982) *Inservice Education and Training of Teachers: a Condition for Education and Change*. Paris: OECD.

Bolam, R. *et al.* (1978) *LEA Advisers and the Mechanism of Innovation*. Slough: NFER.

Boydell, D. (1980) 'The Organisation of Junior School Classrooms: a follow-up survey'. *Educational Research*, **23**: 14–19.

CACE (1967) *Children and their Primary Schools* (The Plowden Report). London: HMSO.

Caldwell, B. J. & Spinks, J. M. (1988) *The Self-Managing School*. Lewes: Falmer Press.

Campbell, R. J. (1985) *Developing the Primary School Curriculum*. London: Holt, Rinehart & Winston.

Carlson, R. E. (1971) 'Effect of Interview Information in Altering Valid Impressions'. *Journal of Applied Psychology*, **55**, 1: 66–72.

Clerkin, C. (1985) 'What do Primary Heads Actually Do All Day'. *School Organization*, **5** (4): 287–300.

Clift, P. S. *et al.* (eds) (1987) *Studies in School Self-Evaluation*. Lewes: Falmer Press.

Coopers & Lybrand (1988) *Local Management of Schools: A Report to the Department of Education and Science*. London: HMSO.

Coulson, A. (1976) 'The Role of the Primary Head' in Peters, R. S. (ed) (1976) *The Role of the Head*. London: Routledge & Kegan Paul.

Coulson, A. (1987) 'Recruitment and Management Development for Primary Headship' in Southworth, G. (ed) (1987) *Readings in Primary School Management*. Lewes: Falmer Press.

Cross Report (1888) 'Report of the Royal Commission on the Elementary Education Acts' in Maclure, J. S. (ed) (1973) *Educational Documents England and Wales*. London: Methuen.

David, M. E. (1977) *Reform, Reaction and Resources*. Slough: NFER.

Davies, L. (1987) 'The Role of the Primary School Head'. *Educational Management & Administration*, **15**: 43–47.

Deal, T. (1985) 'The Symbolism of Effective Schools', in Westoby, A. (ed) (1988) *Culture and Power in Educational Organizations*. Milton Keynes: Open University Press.

Derricott, R. (ed) (1985) *Curriculum Continuity: Primary to Secondary*. Windsor: NFER-Nelson.

DES (1975) *A Language for Life* (The Bullock Report). London: HMSO.

DES (1978) *Primary Education in England*. London: HMSO.

DES (1978) *Special Educational Needs* (The Warnock Report). London: HMSO.

DES (1979) *Management Review of the Department of Education and Science: a report of the Steering Committee*. London: DES.

DES (1982) *Mathematics Counts* (The Cockcroft Report). London: HMSO.

DES (1982) *Study of HM Inspectorate in England and Wales* (The Rayner Report). London: HMSO.

DES (1983) *HM Inspectors Today: standards in education*. London: DES.

DES (1984) *Education Observed*. London: DES.

DES (1985) *Better Schools*. London: HMSO.

DES (1985) *The Curriculum From 5 to 16*. London: HMSO.

DES (1986) *Reporting Inspections: HMI Methods and Procedures, Maintained Schools*.London: DES.

DES (1987) *Primary Schools: some aspects of good practice*. London: HMSO.

DES (1987) *Report by Her Majesty's Inspectors on LEA Provision for Education and the Quality of Response in Schools and Colleges in England 1986*. London: DES.

DES (1987) *Ten Good Schools*. London: HMSO.

DES/Welsh Office (1977) *A new partnership for our schools* (The Taylor Report). London: HMSO.

DES/Welsh Office (1984) *Parental Influence at School: a new framework for school government in England and Wales*. London, HMSO.

DES/Welsh Office (1987) *The National Curriculum 5–16: a consultation document*. London: DES/Welsh Office.

DES/Welsh Office (1988) *Science for Ages 5 to 16: Proposals of the Secretary of State for Education and Science and the Secretary of State for Wales*. London: DES/Welsh Office.

Douglas, J. W. B. (1964) *The Home and the School*. London: MacGibbon & Kee.

Downes, P. (ed) (1988) *Local Financial Management in Schools*. Oxford: Blackwell.

Earley, P. (ed) (1988) *Governors' Reports and Annual Parents' Meetings: the 1988 Education Act and Beyond*. Slough: NFER.

Easen, P. (1985) *Making School-centred INSET Work*. Beckenham: Open University Press/Croom Helm.

Ebbs, B. (1987) 'Internal Review and Development' in Craig, I. (ed) (1987) *Primary School Management in Action*. London: Longman.

Everard, K. B. & Morris, G. (1985) *Effective School Management*. London: Harper & Row.

Fullan, M. G. (1982a) 'Research into Educational Innovation' in Gray, H. L. (ed) (1982) *The Management of Educational Institutions: Theory, Research and Consultancy*. Lewes: Falmer Press.

Fullan, M. G. (1982b) *The Meaning of Educational Change*. New York: Teachers College Press.

Fullan, M. G. (1986) 'The Management of Change' in Hoyle, E. & McMahon, A. (eds) (1986) *The Management of Schools*. London: Kogan Page.

Galton, M. & Willcocks, J. (eds) (1983) *Moving from the Primary Classroom*. London: Routledge & Kegan Paul.

Galton, M. (1983) 'Changing Schools, Changing Teachers' in Smith, L. (ed) (1983) *Changing School: the problems of Transition*. London: University of London, Goldsmiths College.

Galton M. *et al.* (1980) *Inside the Primary Classroom*. London: Routledge & Kegan Paul.

Gilmore, D. C. *et al.* (1986) 'Effects of applicant attractiveness, type of rater and type of job on interview decisions'. *Journal of Occupational Psychology*, **59**: 103–9.

Goodlad, J. I. (1976) *The Dynamics of Educational Change*. New York: McGraw-Hill.

Gray, L. (1984) 'Managing Resources in Schools and Colleges' in Goulding, P. *et al.* (eds) (1984) *Case Studies in Educational Management*. London: Harper & Row.

Greig, D. (1986) 'What do the advisers do all day?' *Education*, **168**(25): 540.

Griffiths, A. & Hamilton, D. (1984) *Parent, Teacher, Child*. London: Methuen.

Gronn, P. C. (1983) 'Talk as the work: the accomplishment of school administration', in Westoby, A. (ed) (1988) *Culture and Power in Educational Organizations*. Milton Keynes: Open University Press.

Hall, V. *et al.* (1986) *Headteachers at Work*. Milton Keynes: Open University Press.

Halpin, A. (1966) *Theory and Research in Administration*. New York: Macmillan.

Handy, C. & Aitken, R. (1986) *Understanding Schools as Organisations*. Harmondsworth: Penguin.

Handy, C. (1985) *Understanding Organisations*. Harmondsworth: Penguin.

Harvey, C.W. (1986) 'How Primary Heads Spend Their Time'. *Educational Management & Administration*, **14**: 60–68.

Havelock, R.G. (1971) *Planning for innovation through dissemination and utilization of knowledge*. Michigan: University of Michigan Centre for Research on Utilization of Scientific Knowledge.

Hemphill, J.K. (1949) *Situational Factors in Leadership*. Columbus: Ohio State University.

Hewison, J. & Tizard, J. (1980) 'Parental Involvement and Reading Attainment'. *British Journal of Educational Psychology*, **50**: 209–215.

Hewton, E. (1988) *School Focused Staff Development*. Lewes: Falmer Press.

Hill, T. (1985) *Managing Financial Resources in Primary Schools: A Case Study*. Unpublished paper: University of Bristol.

Hill, T. (1985) *The Advisory Role: The Perceptions of Primary Heads, Teachers and an Adviser*. Unpublished paper: University of Bristol.

Hodgkinson, C. (1983) *The Philosophy of Leadership*. Oxford: Blackwell.

Hopkins, D. (ed) (1987) *Improving the Quality of Schooling: lessons from the OECD International School Improvement Project*. Lewes: Falmer Press.

House of Commons (1986) *Third Report from the Education, Science and Arts Committee Session 1985–86 'Achievement in Primary Schools' Volume I*. HC 40–1, London: HMSO.

Hoyle, E. (1974) 'Professionality, professionalism and control in Teaching'. *London Educational Review*. **3** (2).

Huberman, A.M. & Miles, M.B. (1984) *Innovation Up Close: How School Improvement Works*. New York: Plenum Press.

Huckman, L. (1988) *The Effects of Local Financial Management on Primary Schools*. Unpublished M.Ed. dissertation: University of Bristol.

ILEA (1977) *Keeping the School Under Review*. London: ILEA.

ILEA (1982) *Keeping the School Under Review*. London: ILEA.

ILEA (1985) *Improving Primary Schools* (The Thomas Report). London: ILEA.

ILEA (1986) *The Junior School Project: A Summary of the Main Report*, London, ILEA. (See also under Mortimore *et al.*, 1988).

Inglis, F. (1985) *The Management of Ignorance: a political theory of the curriculum*. Oxford: Blackwell.

Joyce, B. & Showers, B. (1980) 'Improving Inservice Training: The Messages of Research'. *Educational Leadership*, February 1980, 379–385.

Katz, D. & Kahn, R. L. (1966) *The Social Psychology of Organizations*. New York: John Wiley.

Knight, B. (1983) *Managing School Finance*. London: Heinemann.

Kogan, M. *et al.* (1984) *School Governing Bodies*. London: Heinemann.

Landers, T. & Myers, J. (1977) *Essentials of School Management*. New York: Saunders.

Lawlor, S. (1988) *Opting Out: a guide to why and how*. London: Centre for Policy Studies.

Lawton, D. & Gordon, P. (1987) *HMI*. London: Routledge & Kegan Paul.

Leithwood, K. A. & Montgomery, D. J. (1986) *Improving Principal Effectiveness: The Principal Profile*. Ontario: OISE Press.

Lewin, K. (1944) 'The Dynamics of Group Action'. *Educational Leadership* **1**: 195–200.

Lloyd, K. (1985) 'Management and Leadership in the Primary School' in Hughes, M. *et al.* (eds) (1985) *Managing Education: The System and the Institution*. London: Holt, Rinehart & Winston.

Loucks-Horsley, S. & Hergert, L. F. (1985) *An Action Guide to School Improvement*. Andover: Mass. Association for Supervision and Curriculum Development, The Network.

Lyons, G. (1974) *The Administrative Tasks of Heads and Senior Teachers in Large Secondary Schools*. Bristol: University of Bristol.

Lyons, G. (1976) *Heads' Tasks: a Handbook of secondary school administration*. Windsor: NFER.

Maclure, J. S. (ed) (1965) *Educational Documents in England and Wales 1816 to the present day*. London: Methuen.

McMahon, A. & Bolam, R. (1988) *School Management Development: A Handbook for Primary, Middle and Special Schools*. Bristol: University of Bristol, National Development Centre for School Management Training.

McMahon, A. & Turner, G. (1988) *Staff Development and Appraisal*, E325, *Managing Schools*. Milton Keynes: Open University Press.

McMahon, A. *et al.* (1984) *Guidelines for Review and Internal Development in Schools: Primary School Handbook*. London: Longman/Schools Council.

Measor, L. & Woods, P. (1984) *Changing Schools*. Milton Keynes: Open University Press.

Mintzberg, H. (1973) *The Nature of Managerial Work*. New York: Harper & Row.

Morgan, C. (1986) 'The Selection and Appointment of Heads' in Hoyle, E. & McMahon, A. (eds) (1986) *The Management of Schools*. London: Kogan Page.

Morgan, C. (1988) *Staff Selection in Schools*, E325, *Managing Schools*. Milton Keynes: Open University Press.

Morgan, C. *et al.* (1983) *The Selection of Secondary School Headteachers*. Milton Keynes: Open University Press.

Morgan, C. *et al.* (1984) *A Handbook on Selecting Senior Staff for Schools*. Milton Keynes: Open University Press.

Mortimore, P. *et al.* (1988) *School Matters*. Wells, Open Books (Reports and discusses the findings of the ILEA *Junior School Project*.)

Nash, R. (1973) *Classrooms Observed: the teacher's perceptions of pupil performance*. London: Routledge and Kegan Paul.

NDC (1988) *Consortium of School Teacher Appraisal Pilot Schemes, Progress on Appraisal: interim report*. Bristol: University of Bristol, National Development Centre for School Management and Training.

Nias, J. (1980) 'Leadership Styles and Job Satisfaction' in Bush, T. *et al.* (eds) (1980) *Approaches to School Management*. London, Harper & Row/Oxford University Press.

Nias, J. *et al.* (forthcoming) *Understanding the Primary School as an Organisation*. London: Cassell.

Nicholls, A. (1983) *Managing Educational Innovations*. London: Harper & Row.

Oldroyd, D. *et al.* (1984) *School-based Staff Development Activities*. London: Schools Council/Longman.

Perry, P. (1987) 'The Secret Gardeners'. *Times Educational Supplement*, 10/7/87: 22.

Persell, C. H. & Cookson, P. W. (1982) *The Effective Principal: a research summary*. Reston: NASSP.

Peters, J. J. & Waterman, R. H. (1982) *In Search of Excellence*. London: Harper & Row.

Reid, K. *et al.* (1987) *Towards the Effective School*. Oxford: Blackwell.

Rendell, M. (1968) *Graduate Administrators in Local Education Authorities*. London: University of London Institute of Education.

Richards, C. (1986) 'The Curriculum from 5 to 16: Background, Content and some Implications for Primary Education' in Southworth, G. (ed) (1987) *Readings in Primary School Management*. Lewes: Falmer Press.

Salaman, G. & Thompson, K. (1974) *The Sociology of Interviews* DT352 *People and Organizations*. Milton Keynes: Open University Press.

Schmuck, P.A. (1986) 'School Management and Administration: an analysis by gender' in Hoyle, E. & McMahon, A. (eds) (1986) *The Management of Schools*. London: Kogan Page.

Sergiovanni, J. T. (1984) 'Leadership and Excellence in Schooling'. *Educational Leadership*, February: 4–13.

Southworth, G. (1987) 'Staff Selection or By Appointment? A Case Study of the Appointment of a Teacher to a Primary School' in Southworth, G (ed) (1987) *Readings in Primary School Mangement*. Lewes: Falmer Press.

Stenner, A. (1987) 'School-centred Financial Management' in Craig, I. (ed) (1987) *Primary School Management in Action*. London: Longman.

Stewart, R. (1967) *Managers and their Jobs*. London: Macmillan.

Stillman, A. & Grant, M. (1988) *A Study of the LEA Advisory Service*. Windsor: NFER-Nelson.

Stillman, A. & Maychell, K. (1984) *School to School*. Windsor: NFER-Nelson.

Stogdill, R. (1974) *Handbook of Leadership: A Survey of Theory and Research*. New York: Free Press.

Taylor, P. (1986) *Expertise and the Primary School Teacher*. Windsor: NFER-Nelson.

Thomas, H. (1987) 'Efficiency and Opportunity in School Finance Autonomy' in Thomas, H. & Simkins, T. (eds) (1987) *Economics and the Management of Education: Emerging Themes*. Lewes: Falmer Press.

Thomas, N. (1983) 'HM Inspectorate' in Open University (1983) E364 *Curriculum Evaluation and Assessment in Educational Institutions*, Block 2, Part 3, *Approaches to Evaluation: Inspections*. Milton Keynes: Open University Press.

Tizard, B. *et al.* (1981) *Involving Parents in Nursery and Infant Schools*. London: Grant McIntyre.

Van Gennep, A. (1960) *The Rites of Passage*. London: Routledge & Kegan Paul.

Walker, R. (1981) *The Observational Work of Local Authority Inspectors and Advisers*. Norwich: University of East Anglia, Centre for Applied Research in Education.

Webster, E. C. (1964) *Decision Making in the Employment Interview*. Montreal: McGill University, Industrial Relations Center.

Weindling, D. & Earley, P. (1987) *Secondary Headship: The First Years*. Windsor: NFER-Nelson.

Welsh Office (1986) *A Survey of Links Between Primary and Secondary Schools*. Cardiff: Welsh Office.

Wilcox, B. 'Clarifying The Role of the Adviser'. *Education*, **167**. 331.

Winkley, D. (1985) *Diplomats and detectives: LEA Advisers at Work*. London: Robert Royce.

Wolcott, H. F. (1973 reissued 1984) *The Man in the Principal's Office*. Prospect Heights, Illinois: Waveland Press.

Youngman, M. B. (ed) (1986) *Mid-Schooling Transfer: Problems and Proposals*. Windsor: NFER-Nelson.

Index

To, Dear Vathsala

with Love + Best Wishes,

[illegible] - 6/3/99
(Mrs. Thomas)

17